Contents

D1331461

Introduction

Aims of the guide

The purpose of this Student Text Guide to *The Tempest* is to enable you to organise your thoughts and responses to the play, to deepen your understanding of key features and aspects, and to help you to address the particular requirements of examination questions in order to obtain the best possible grade. It will also prove useful to those of you writing a coursework piece on the play by providing summaries, lists, analyses and references to help with the content and construction of the assignment. Line references in this guide refer to the *New Penguin Shakespeare* edition of the play.

The remainder of this Introduction consists of exam board Assessment Objectives and a revision scheme which gives a suggested programme for using the material in the guide. There is also a section offering practical advice on writing examination essays.

The Text Guidance section consists of a series of subsections which examine key aspects of the play including contexts, interpretations and controversies. Emboldened terms within the Text Guidance section are glossed in 'Literary terms and concepts' on pp. 80–85.

The final section, Questions and Answers, includes mark schemes, exemplar essay plans and samples of marked work.

Assessment Objectives

The Assessment Objectives (AOs) for A-level English Literature are common to all boards:

AO1	communicate clearly the knowledge, understanding and insight appropriate to literary study, using appropriate terminology and accurate and coherent written expression
AO2i	respond with knowledge and understanding to literary texts of different types and periods
AO2ii	respond with knowledge and understanding to literary texts of different types and periods, exploring and commenting on relationships and comparisons between literary texts
AO3	show detailed understanding of the ways in which writers' choices of form, structure and language shape meanings
AO4	articulate independent opinions and judgements, informed by different interpretations of literary texts by other readers

AO5i	show understanding of the contexts in which literary texts are written and understood
AO5ii	evaluate the significance of cultural, historical and other contextual influences on literary texts and study

A summary and paraphrase of each Assessment Objective is given below and would be worth memorising:

AO1	clarity of written communication
AO2	informed personal response in relation to time and genre (literary context)
AO3	the creative literary process (context of writing)
AO4	critical and interpretative response (context of reading)
AO5	evaluation of influences (cultural context)

The Tempest has a total weighting of 20–30%, divided as follows:

OCR	AO1 – 5%; AO3 – 5%; AO4 – 10%; AO5i – 10% Total – 30%
Edexcel	AO2ii – 10%; AO4 – 5%; AO5ii – 5% Total – 20%
AQA Spec A	AO1 – 8%; AO2i – 10%; AO3 – 7%; AO4 – 5% Total – 30%

Note the different weighting of Assessment Objectives between the different examining boards for the same text. It is essential that you pay close attention to the AOs, and their weighting, for the board for which you are entered. These are what the examiner will be looking for, and you must address them *directly* and *specifically*, in addition to proving general familiarity with and understanding of the text, and being able to present an argument clearly, relevantly and convincingly.

Remember the examiners are seeking above all else evidence of an *informed personal response* to the text. A revision guide such as this can help you to understand the text and to form your own opinions, and can suggest areas to think about, but it cannot replace your own ideas and responses as an individual reader.

Revision advice

For the examined units it is possible that either brief or more extensive revision will be necessary because the original study of the text took place some time previously. It is therefore as well to know how to go about revising and which tried and tested methods are considered the most successful for literature exams at all levels, from GCSE to degree finals.

There are no short cuts to effective exam revision; the only one way to know a text well, and to know your way around it in an exam, is to have done the necessary studying. If you use the following six-stage method for both open- and closed-book revision, you will not only revisit and reassess all your previous work on the text in a manageable way but will be able to distil, organise and retain your knowledge.

(1) Between a month and a fortnight before the exam, depending on your schedule (a simple list of stages with dates to display in your room, not a work of art!), you will need to reread the text, this time taking stock of all the underlinings and marginal annotations as well. As you read, collect onto sheets of A4 the essential ideas and quotations as you come across them. The acts of selecting key material and recording it as notes are natural ways of stimulating thought and aiding memory.

(2) Reread the highlighted areas and marginal annotations in your critical extracts and background handouts, and add anything useful from them to your list of notes and quotations. Then reread your previous essays and the teacher's comments. As you look back through essays written earlier in the course, you should have the pleasant sensation of realising that you could now write much better on the text than you could then. You will also discover that much of your huge file of notes is redundant or repeated, and that you have changed your mind about some beliefs, so that the distillation process is not too daunting. Selecting what is important is the way to crystallise your knowledge and understanding.

(3) During the run-up to the exam you need to do lots of practice essay plans to help you identify any gaps in your knowledge and give you practice in planning in 5–8 minutes. Past paper titles for you to plan are provided in this guide, some of which can be done as full timed essays — and marked strictly according to exam criteria — which will show whether length and timing are problematic for you. If you have not seen a copy of a real exam paper before you take your first module, ask to see a past paper so that you are familiar with the layout, rubric and types of question. For each text you are studying for the examination you need to know exactly which Assessment Objectives are being tested and where the heaviest weighting falls, as well as whether it is a closed- or open-book exam. It would also be helpful if your teacher shared with you the examiners' reports on past papers.

(4) About a week before the exam, reduce your two or three sides of A4 notes to a double-sided postcard of very small, dense writing. Collect a group of key words by once again selecting and condensing, and use abbreviations for quotations (first and last word), and character and place names (initials). Choosing and writing out the short quotations will help you to focus on the essential issues, and to recall them quickly in the exam. Make sure that your selection covers the main themes and includes examples of imagery, language, style, comments on character, examples of

irony and other significant aspects of the text. Previous class discussion and essay writing will have indicated which quotations are useful for almost any title; pick those which can serve more than one purpose. In this way a minimum number of quotations can have maximum application.

(5) You now have in a compact, accessible form all the material for any possible essay title. There are only half a dozen themes relevant to a literary text so if you have covered these, you should not meet with any nasty surprises when you read the exam questions. You don't need to refer to your file of paperwork again, or even to the text. For the few days before the exam, you can read through your handy postcard whenever and wherever you get the opportunity. Each time you read it, which will only take a few minutes, you are reminding yourself of all the information you will be able to recall in the exam to adapt to the general title or to support an analysis of particular passages.

(6) A fresh, active mind works wonders, and information needs time to settle, so don't try to cram just before the exam. Get a good night's sleep the night before. Then you will be able to enter the exam room with all the confidence of a well-prepared candidate.

Coursework

It is possible that you are doing *The Tempest* as a Shakespeare or other coursework text. If so, you must be sure that your title(s), negotiated with your teacher, fits the Assessment Objectives and their respective weighting for your board. Coursework for all boards must be between 1,500 and 2,000 words. If you are obliged to, or choose to, write two pieces (depending on the board), consideration will need to be given to how the two relate to each other and cover different aspects of the text without overlap. The coursework writing process differs from an examination in being more leisurely and more supported by the discussion and drafting stages, but the issues of the text remain the same, as does the need for a relevant, focused response to the title.

Coursework should be word-processed in the interests of presentation, consideration for the examiner, and ease of alteration for the student. There are a number of key stages in the coursework writing process:

- Once your title is decided and you are familiar with the Assessment Objectives, reread the play and all the notes and annotations you have made, extracting what is relevant for your title.
- With teacher guidance, read some background material and critical essays, and collect any relevant information from them. Keep a list of the books and articles you have consulted. Rephrase any ideas you borrow from elsewhere.
- Write a one-page essay plan, consisting of subheadings and main points, and show it to your teacher to ensure you have covered the title fully and have adopted an appropriate essay structure.

- Write a draft of the essay, roughly the right length, based on your plan. Use details, examples and quotations from the text to support your points.
- Read through the draft, making sure that you have answered fully and remained focused on the question. Submit your draft to your teacher in good time.
- When your draft is returned, put into practice the comments offered to help you improve your essay and its grade, and adjust the length if necessary.
- Produce the final version, improving content, expression and accuracy where possible. Check the final word count. Include a bibliography listing the texts you have quoted from or consulted in your writing of your essay.
- After a final read through, putting yourself in the position of the reader, make last-minute adjustments and submit your essay — before the deadline.

Writing examination essays

Essay content

One of the key skills you are being asked to demonstrate at A-level is the ability to select and tailor your knowledge of the text and its background to the question set in the exam paper. In order to reach the highest levels, you need to avoid 'pre-packaged' essays which lack focus, relevance and coherence, and which simply contain everything you know about the text. Be ruthless in rejecting irrelevant material, after considering whether it can be made relevant by a change of emphasis. Aim to cover the whole question, not just part of it; your response needs to demonstrate breadth and depth, covering the full range of text elements: character, event, theme and language. Only half a dozen essay approaches are possible for any set text, though they may be phrased in a variety of ways, and they are likely to refer to the key themes of the text. Preparation of the text therefore involves extensive discussion and practice at manipulating these core themes so that there should be no surprises in the exam. An apparently new angle is more likely to be something familiar presented in an unfamiliar way and you should not panic or reject the choice of question because you think you know nothing about it.

Exam titles are open-ended in the sense that there is no obvious right answer, and you would therefore be unwise to give a dismissive, extreme or entirely one-sided response; the question would not have been set if the answer were not debatable. An ability and willingness to see both sides is an Assessment Objective and shows independence of judgement as a reader. Don't be afraid to explore the issues and don't try to tie the text into one neat interpretation. If there is ambiguity it is likely to be deliberate on the part of the author and must be discussed; literary texts are complex and often paradoxical, and it would be a misreading of them to suggest that there is only one possible interpretation. You are not expected, however, to argue equally strongly or extensively for both sides of an argument, since personal opinion is an important factor. It is advisable to deal with the alternative view at the beginning of your response, and then construct your own view as the main part of the essay. This makes it less likely that you will appear to cancel out your own line of argument.

Choosing the right question

The first skill you must show when presented with the exam paper is the ability to choose the better, for you, of the two questions on your text where there is a choice. This is not to say you should always go for the same type of essay (whole-text or passage-based), and if the question is not one which you feel happy with for any reason you should seriously consider the other, even if it is not the type you normally prefer. It is unlikely, but still possible, that a question contains a word you are not sure you know the meaning of, in which case it would be safer to choose the other one.

Don't be tempted to choose a question because of its similarity to one you have already done. Freshness and thinking on the spot usually produce a better product than attempted recall of a previous essay that may have received only a mediocre mark in the first place. The exam question is unlikely to have exactly the same focus and your response may seem 'off centre' as a result, as well as stale and perfunctory in expression.

Essay questions fall into the following categories: close section analysis and relation to whole text; characterisation; setting and atmosphere; structure and effectiveness; genre; language and style; themes and issues. Remember, however, that themes are relevant to all essays and that analysis, not just description, is always required.

Once you have decided which exam question to attempt, follow the procedure below for whole-text and passage-based, open- and closed-book essays.

(1) Underline all the key words in the question and note how many parts the question has.

(2) Plan your answer, using aspects of the key words and parts of the question as subheadings, in addition to themes. Aim for 10–12 ideas. Check that the Assessment Objectives are covered.

(3) Support your argument by selecting the best examples of characters, events, imagery and quotations to prove your points. Remove ideas for which you can find no evidence.

(4) Structure your answer by grouping and numbering your points in a logical progression. Identify the best general point to keep for the conclusion.

(5) Introduce your essay with a short paragraph setting the context and defining the key words in the question as broadly, but relevantly, as possible.

(6) Write the rest of the essay, following your structured plan but adding extra material if it occurs to you. Paragraph your writing and consider expression, especially sentence structure and vocabulary choices, as you write. Signal changes in the direction of your argument with paragraph openers such as 'Furthermore' and 'However'. Use plenty of short, integrated quotations and use the words of the text rather than your own where possible. Use technical terms appropriately, and write concisely and precisely, avoiding vagueness and ambiguity.

(7) Your conclusion should sound conclusive and make it clear that you have answered the question. It should be an overview of the question and the text, not a repetition or a summary of points already made.

(8) Cross out your plan with a neat diagonal line.

(9) Check your essay for content, style, clarity and accuracy. With neat crossings-out, correct errors of fact, spelling, grammar and punctuation. Improve expression if possible, and remove any repetition and irrelevance. Add clarification and missing evidence, if necessary, using omission marks or asterisks. Even at this stage good new material can be added.

There is no such thing as a perfect or model essay; flawed essays can gain full marks. There is always something more which could have been said, and examiners realise that students have limitations when writing under pressure in timed conditions. You are not penalised for what you didn't say in comparison to some idealised concept of the perfect answer, but rewarded for the knowledge and understanding you have shown. It is not as difficult as you may think to do well, provided that you know the text in detail and have sufficient essay-writing experience. Follow the process of **choose**, **underline**, **select**, **support**, **structure**, **write** and **check**, and you can't go far wrong.

Text Guidance

Contexts

The England of the early 1600s had just undergone a radical change of monarch and was involved in ambitious ventures of discovery and colonial expansion. The new century brought challenges to the Elizabethan world view inherited from the Middle Ages, and this conflict is represented in the drama of the period.

Cultural context

Below are some of the contemporary religious beliefs and social attitudes which throw light on the hopes, fears, thoughts and actions of the characters in *The Tempest*, and which Shakespeare exploits while simultaneously calling them into question.

Chain of being

The Elizabethans inherited from medieval theology the concept of a hierarchical chain of being on which every creature appeared in its ordained position on a ladder descending from God through angel, king, man and woman (in that order) to animal, vegetable and, finally, mineral. This belief in a divine order was often used to explain the innate inferiority of women to men, thereby maintaining the status quo in the patriarchal societies of Elizabethan and Jacobean England. *The Tempest*, however, is philosophically daring in that it opens up many important debates about the chain of being. There are several instances in the play where we are asked to question what a man is, and whether a hierarchical system of categorising one man as better than another is necessarily reliable. In the storm scene at the start of the play the Boatswain declares all men aboard the ship as equal in the face of the pounding waves, asking: 'What cares these roarers for the name of king?' (I.1.16–17). Though a slave, Caliban speaks with much greater dignity and beauty in his **verse** than either Stephano or Trinculo can muster in their drunken outpourings, which are usually delivered in prose (a form generally reserved by Shakespeare for 'lower' characters).

Gonzalo's philosophical reflection in Act II scene 1 on what constitutes a **utopian** society goes even further, questioning the value of the refinements of culture enjoyed by European civilisation. The introduction of 'progressive' concepts like trade, law and land division are not, in Gonzalo's eyes, necessarily an improvement in human society. Gonzalo thus acts as a mouthpiece for **relativism**, a school of thought which believes that ideas of right and wrong, truth and falsehood differ from place to place, and that there can be no single reliable method of judging the value of any way of life as objectively superior to another. Shakespeare also seems to suggest that moral sensibility is not, as was widely thought at the time, purely a product of social class. The island provides a fascinating **microcosm** in which characters from several different backgrounds — Antonio, Sebastian, Caliban, Stephano and Trinculo — are all willing to attempt a coup against the ruling powers when given the opportunity. (Alonso and Antonio have both already exhibited their ambition by deposing Prospero as Duke of Milan before the play begins.) Furthermore, it was believed that the failure to apply reason reduced humans to the animal state of being governed by appetite and instinct; in Shakespeare, a human who falls below the level of man into the realm of bestiality is labelled a monster. The presence of Caliban — a 'reasonable' monster, in contrast to some of the 'monstrous' human characters — is therefore particularly thought-provoking; Prospero's assertion at the end of the play that 'He [Caliban] is as disproportioned in his manners/As in his shape' (V.1.291–92) is not, perhaps, altogether convincing. Caliban's sophisticated use of language certainly belies his bestial appearance.

Nature

The ubiquity of the word 'Nature' in Elizabethan literature, and of **imagery** deriving from it and arguments about it, stems from the contemporary debate about the definition of Nature, which has two contradictory aspects: the benevolent and harmonious, in contrast to the wild and violent. In Act II scene 1 Gonzalo states that 'nature should bring forth' and supply his ideal society (165), implicitly condemning the artificial way he and his contemporaries live in Europe. Shakespeare also plays with the **paradox** of the existence of unnatural monsters, which could only have been bred by Nature and must, therefore, be natural in some sense. The human struggle to impose nurture, by cultivating and refining natural forces, is personified in the character of Caliban, who is initially befriended and taught to speak by Miranda and Prospero, but is then enslaved by his teachers after he transgresses their laws. Prospero is certainly frustrated by what he sees as his lack of success in 'civilising' Caliban, as he calls him 'A devil, a born devil, on whose nature/Nurture can never stick' (IV.1.188–89).

The New World and slavery

The character of Caliban is certainly extremely important in relation to the recent European discovery of the New World. Christopher Columbus made his first voyage to the Americas in 1492 and English colonies were established soon afterwards. The attitude of cultural superiority brought by the Europeans, however, often led to the country's indigenous peoples being treated cruelly or enslaved. As touched on above, it is a matter of debate whether Caliban is an ungrateful beneficiary of Prospero and Miranda's colonisation of the island, or an oppressed native who has been forced to bow to foreign aggressors.

The slavery industry was closely linked to colonisation and is implicated in the way we view the play. The visit to London by the black-skinned ambassador of the King of Barbary in 1600–01 caused a stir in society and, many critics claim, provided

considerable material for the composition of *Othello*. At a time when world travel was unknown to all but a few hardened seafarers, images of the 'other' sparked a mixture of curiosity and fear. As Trinculo notes in Act II scene 2, the citizens of England 'will not give a doit to relieve a lame beggar' but 'will lay out ten to see a dead Indian' (31–32). White Europe's fascination with and exploitation of alien races was not, however, a one-way experience. There are several reports of white explorers from Europe being attacked and kidnapped while visiting foreign lands, and being confined in harsh conditions and other mistreatment; occurrences to which Sebastian alludes when chastising Alonso for letting his daughter Claribel marry the King of Tunis.

Appearance

External appearance was believed by many in Chaucer's and Shakespeare's time to be an indicator of what lay within (i.e. goodness or evil). Beauty and whiteness were associated with what is fair, ugliness and blackness with what was foul. Caliban is described as a 'thing of darkness' (V.1.275) while Ferdinand is so handsome that Miranda is tempted to call him 'A thing divine' (I.2.419) as soon as she lays eyes on him. A physical deformity was thought to be the devil's mark and took many women to the stake. Prospero punishes Caliban's attempted rape of Miranda particularly severely, displaying a fear of miscegenation (racial impurity caused by sex between different races). This theme is echoed in *Othello*, when Brabantio hears of Desdemona's marriage to the black general Othello, and exclaims 'O treason of the blood!' (I.1.185). The tension between appearance and reality is also a central issue in *The Tempest*. By the end of the play Gonzalo and Alonso in particular are so shocked by the stream of revelations made by Prospero — a man they both took to be dead — that they barely trust their own eyes to inform them of what is happening. Given the magician's control of magic and illusion, it is no surprise that the imagery of 'seeming' permeates the language of this play (as well as of many other Shakespeare dramas). Indeed, Prospero's speech (IV.1.156–58), where he asserts that

> We are such stuff
> As dreams are made on; and our little life
> Is rounded with a sleep

works in combination with the Epilogue to highlight the illusory nature of the theatre, and of life itself; he seems, in fact, to be questioning the very idea of what is real and what is not.

Reason

The failure of reason was considered to be the cause of the Fall of Man (Adam allowed his love for Eve to overrule his better judgement and obedience to God), and Elizabethans therefore believed it was dangerous to let reason be dominated by passion, or any other impulse. Characters in Shakespeare who become uncontrollably emotional are heading for a fall, as their intellect is what makes them human (superior to beasts) and keeps them sane. Stephano and Trinculo submit to the disorientating influence of alcohol before being joined by Caliban. This sub-plot raises many questions about which characters are the most bestial of the cast, particularly given that Caliban later renounces the bottle and the 'dull fool' whom he worshipped under its influence (V.1.298).

Machiavelli

Machiavelli was an Italian who in 1513 wrote a book called *The Prince*, which advocated self-interest as a means of political advancement. His philosophy, which recommends the ruthless eradication of one's enemies, is adopted by several of Shakespeare's villains, including Antonio and Sebastian. Looking after one's own interests and eschewing the precepts of Christianity and fatalism is justified by the amoral Machiavels as the only logical and effective way to proceed in life. For them the end justifies the means, and guilt and repentance are for foolish weaklings. It is interesting that Prospero rejects such duplicitous political strategies at the end of the play, hoping that he has taught his would-be usurpers an unforgettable lesson. Critics have debated the wisdom of this judgement, with some labelling his actions naïve while others prefer to view them as magnanimous.

Courtly love

Romance in Shakespeare's time was reflected in the **genre** of **courtly love**, represented in *The Tempest* by Ferdinand and Miranda's relationship. Ferdinand is a handsome prince, and Miranda is the rightful heir to the throne of Milan. Their relationship unfolds quickly, but it is characterised by Ferdinand's chivalrous manners and poetic language, as he (unlike Caliban) gladly suffers the indignity of carrying wood for Prospero because of the time it affords him with Miranda. She, in turn, offers to lighten his load, displaying compassion and sympathy for the man she loves. Whether or not he decides to marry her, Miranda swears her fidelity to him — another traditional **motif** of the romance. The female object of affection in courtly romance was also expected to have rival suitors competing for her hand, which — in a slightly unconventional way — could be represented in Stephano's desire to take her as his queen and, perhaps, Caliban's early attempt to rape her. In addition to love affairs romance concerned exotic tales of magic, superstition and travel to distant parts, and brought together the masculine ideals of the soldier and the lover, as in the Arthurian legends. By definition the courtly lover had to be a member of high society and concerned above all with the notions of honour and reputation.

The role of women

Students might wonder at the insistence on female chastity in so many Shakespeare plays. The security of society and peace of mind of men was dependent upon women's virginity before marriage — making them a bargaining tool for advantageous marriages to benefit the father's social status — and chastity after it, meaning faithfulness to their husbands. Ferdinand asks Miranda if she is a maid, effectively implying that he cannot marry her if she is not. In a society which passed inheritance down the male line, men needed to be sure that their son was really their own and not someone else's bastard, and a man's reputation would be destroyed by an unfaithful wife. Virginity and chastity were linked to religion via the Virgin Mary and regarded not only as an ideal state for women but as a test of the nobility of males, since only the higher orders were thought to be able to resist the temptations of the flesh (hence Prospero's strictures on the subject to Ferdinand just before the masque scene in Act IV scene 1). It should be noted, however, that only-child daughters in Shakespeare often tend to be more rebellious. This may be due to their assuming some masculine roles in the absence of a male heir (as Elizabeth I did when she ascended the throne).

Women were possessions, financially dependent on their fathers, to whom they owed obedience and domestic labour, until they were handed over to the rule of their husbands, whom they had to love, honour and obey, as well as allow their conjugal rights. The consequences of not performing these daughterly and wifely duties were serious, involving being disowned and deprived of a home, financial support and a place in society. Prospero is certainly an authoritarian father to Miranda, delivering stern lectures and engineering her relationship with Ferdinand. However, there is no reason to disbelieve his claim to her that he has 'done nothing but in care of thee' (I.2.16). The nature of their secluded life on the island means that they are free of the scrutiny of public opinion, and in this sense it is hardly surprising that Miranda has grown into a woman who is slightly atypical of her time. She breaks her father's commandment not to tell Ferdinand her name and is actually the first to raise the idea of marriage, rather than waiting for him to propose. For all her strength of character, however, Miranda still finds herself subject to the demands of the men around her.

Evil spirits

Evil spirits were believed to be permanently within earshot and on the watch for an opportunity to corrupt and snatch a human soul from the pathway of righteousness. For instance, Hamlet wonders whether the ghostly form of his father which he sees at the start of that play is an incarnation of a devil who is trying to secure his damnation. All magic was considered suspicious and there was no clear distinction between 'white' (good) and 'black' (bad) magic. James I wrote a book on witchcraft and the supernatural entitled *Daemonologie*, and he was categorical that magic was a force for evil. Although Ariel's spirits initially appear good to the courtiers as they present a luxurious feast to them in Act III scene 3, they quickly remove the victuals and Sebastian proceeds to run after them, with the intention of killing 'one fiend at a time' (104). Even apparently benevolent magical forces were often considered to be evil spirits who had acquired a deceptive outer appearance of goodness to work their satanic ends. A Jacobean audience would have had a suspicious attitude to Prospero's magic and it is therefore no surprise that he breaks his staff and discards his magic books by the end of the play.

Alchemy

Alchemy was the supposedly scientific study of turning base metal (like lead) into gold, which was still practised in the seventeenth century. Shakespeare's contemporary Ben Jonson even wrote a play based around this pursuit (*The Alchemist*, first acted in 1610). Although Jonson sought to satirise those who believed they could make a fortune in this way, the practice was not entirely scientifically discredited, as it is today. For some alchemists, the practice also contained elements of mysticism; the genesis of a new, more valuable substance from relatively worthless ingredients allowed them to feel that they were changing the very fabric of the world, giving them godlike power. In this sense, Prospero's relationship with Caliban carries overtones of alchemy, as the magician attempts to turn a base man into a 'civilised' human being. Likewise, the magician's actions at the end of the play suggest that he is hoping to transform 'evil' characters into 'good' ones by showing them forgiveness. In this sense, Prospero shows the hubris of a character who assumes the power of a god to effect changes in others.

Historical context

Discovering new worlds

The '**Golden Age**' of discovery was in full swing by the time Shakespeare wrote *The Tempest*, and the play is clearly influenced by some of the remarkable voyages made by travellers and seafarers during the sixteenth and seventeenth centuries. Although America was inhabited long before the arrival of Europeans, and was possibly discovered by the Chinese centuries earlier than 1492, the adventures of Christopher Columbus sparked a great increase in the number of foreign trips made by European explorers. Enterprising traders realised what profits could be made by shipping goods from abroad, and set off for distant lands with the aim of making their fortunes by trading exotic commodities.

Sea travel in Shakespeare's time was not the relatively safe endeavour it is today. Some sailors placed large sums of money with insurers on the understanding that it would be paid back many times over if they returned home alive with proof

of their travels. The large number of men who failed to do so made this a profitable business for such insurers. As a result, the seas came to represent chance, fortune and fate. Antonio in *The Merchant of Venice* gambles his fortune on the waves and is seemingly left destitute when his ships do not return to port on time. Likewise, Mariana in *Measure for Measure* is left destitute after her brother's ship is lost at sea, leading to her rejection by her betrothed, Angelo.

The increase in international exploration also led to the publication of many pamphlets documenting the peoples and countries encountered by the voyagers. Some contained exaggeration and fiction, but they nevertheless provide a very useful insight into the way explorers perceived the New World. Shakespeare almost certainly read a number of these publications, using many of the images and stories from them as **sources** for *The Tempest*.

Christopher Columbus

Columbus's journal is just one of several invaluable works that documented the life of a European traveller at sea. In it he writes of his adventures in distant lands, meeting 'friendly' indigenous peoples who were fascinated by the Europeans' clothing and trinkets. He comments on their face and body painting, and compliments them for being 'handsomely formed' and 'ingenious' people. However, such praise is tempered by Columbus's assumption of innate superiority to these people: as far as he is concerned, their fine quality means that they 'would be good servants' rather than allies. Columbus's attitude reflects the English view of foreign cultures as potential resources rather than as autonomous systems worthy of respect.

One of the main reasons for this superior tone was the difference in religion between the Christian European explorers and the 'heathen' natives they met. The first English colonies were set up as a means of 'educating' foreigners in matters of religion in particular, spreading Christianity to far-flung outposts across the sea. Plantations there provided the ideal opportunity to combine missionary zeal with great business acumen.

Relations between the indigenous Americans and their European visitors often became strained as an atmosphere of mutual distrust built up. Columbus himself reported that he captured several of the tribespeople he encountered in order to bring them back to Europe and teach them English. He also makes several comments in his writing which refer to the possibility of fortifying some of the islands he discovered, and to the ease with which the indigenous people could be suppressed. Subsequent trips by such famous characters as Sir Francis Drake and Sir Walter Raleigh cemented the reputation of ground-breaking English explorers who brought back exotic crops such as potatoes and tobacco. However, one person's pioneer is another person's pirate; European domination over the New World led not only to the oppression of many indigenous peoples, but also to the escalation of tension between the main European powers, who vied for the control of resources in the colonies.

Richard Hakluyt

In addition to reading pamphlets which documented contemporary foreign travels, there is now overwhelming critical consensus that Shakespeare studied the works of Richard Hakluyt as a means of researching details about seafaring expeditions. The first of Hakluyt's writings, *Divers Voyages*, appeared in 1582. He subsequently made several adventurous journeys, cataloguing his findings and trawling others' accounts to produce works such as *Principall Navigations* (1589). The works of Hakluyt had the effect of stimulating interest in foreign travel and colonisation, as well as encouraging English scientists to increase their knowledge of astronomy and navigation.

One of Hakluyt's main motivations was to break down the culture of secrecy about new lands, which had been built up by merchants reluctant to disclose details of their discoveries in case others should benefit from them. He set about redressing this situation by undertaking and documenting journeys with no explicit commercial goal.

The Tempest was written against a backdrop of nautical adventure, discovery and growing imperialism. Shipwrecks and distant, exotic lands captured the public imagination and seem to have made the play an instant hit. The increasing colonisation of foreign lands, the cultural and religious arrogance of the colonists, as well as the oppression of previously independent peoples, are all worth considering when studying *The Tempest*. As well as reflecting the political climate of the time, the tensions between Prospero and Caliban — and indeed between all of the characters on the island — also provide a fascinating analogue to historical debates about the morality of occupying foreign territories. Even today, when the European colonies have been all but dismantled, the play continues to be relevant to political issues, in particular the interventionist foreign policies of many states.

The 'noble savage'

Michel de Montaigne was a prominent philosopher in the sixteenth century, whose ideas were held great in great respect at the time Shakespeare was writing. In his essay 'Of the Canniballes' (see 'Play context' section), Montaigne writes at length of his travels in Brazil and his encounters with the natives of the country. Although many white Europeans believed that they were innately superior to indigenous peoples of other countries, Montaigne was far more open-minded, concluding that 'there is nothing in that nation, that is either barbarous or savage, unless men call that barbarisme, which is not common to them'. These comments form the basis of Montaigne's concept of the 'noble savage', a man who has not been exposed to the 'civilising' elements of Western society, but who nonetheless retains the nobility of humankind. Shakespeare's characterisation of Caliban is clearly informed by

Montaigne's thinking, and we are invited to explore whether Caliban's upbringing on a remote island makes him inferior to the characters who come from Italy, or just different.

Theatrical context

Shakespeare and contemporary theatre

In the early seventeenth century, when Shakespeare wrote his major tragedies, drama had generally become more political, satirical, violent and tragic compared to the more lyrical tastes and pastoral works of the Elizabethans. There was a growing fashion for the use of masque and spectacle in plays and poetry (as we see in *The Tempest*), and an emphasis on bloodthirsty revenge tragedies in urban settings among fellow playwrights such as Ben Jonson and John Webster. However, wit, **irony** and sophistication of ideas were still paramount in the plots, characterisation and language of the theatre.

Play-going appealed to all sections of the population; the poor stood as 'groundlings' below the raised stage while the wealthier sat in galleries or boxes. King James, a supporter of Shakespeare's company, The King's Men, was a keen theatre-goer with a personal interest in witchcraft, religion and the role of the monarch. Contemporary playwrights catered for these tastes in their choice of subject matter and creation of characters.

All the world's a metatheatre

Above all, Shakespeare understood that the theatre was an artificial construct, and that the gap between the world of the stage and the reality of the auditorium could be explored and exploited. In this sense he embraced the concept of **metatheatre** even before the term had been invented.

Metatheatre is a style of drama which acknowledges and draws attention to the artificiality of the theatre, the dramatic techniques it uses, and the role of the playwright. In *Hamlet*, *The Taming of the Shrew* and *A Midsummer Night's Dream* Shakespeare inserts plays-within-a-play, which distance us from the main action and remind us that what we are watching is a theatrical illusion. One of Shakespeare's contemporaries, Ben Jonson, was extremely adept at subtly reminding his audience that he was in control of the action of the play; at the end of *Volpone*, for example, the eponymous hero addresses the audience in much the same way as Prospero does in his epilogue, asserting that he has done 'no suffering' against us, and asking us to clap in appreciation of his efforts. Both playwrights therefore exhibit an acute understanding of the dynamic between theatre and audience. Similarly, Puck's epilogue at the end of *A Midsummer Night's Dream* reminds us that the play we have been watching is itself an illusion, as he declares in Act V scene 1:

...you have but slumbered here
While these visions did appear,
And this weak and idle theme,
No more yielding but a dream.

The romances

Romance as a genre derives from the word *roman* in Old French, which referred to courtly tales of legends, knights and classical heroes. These works often made use of magical and supernatural elements to create a sense of a fictional world somehow removed from that of everyday life. They were usually a vehicle for conveying a moral message, and (in the English tradition at least) tended to be composed in prose. Romances usually explored the **themes** of love and morality in an idealised setting.

Shakespeare's romances

When the First Folio (the first collected edition of Shakespeare's works) was published in 1623 its plays were divided under the headings of 'Comedies', 'Tragedies' and 'Histories'. *The Tempest* appeared as a comedy, the very first play in the volume. However, this loose and problematic categorisation has been revised over the years. *The Tempest* is now popularly termed a romance, and as such is grouped together with *Pericles* (which did not appear in the original Folio), *The Winter's Tale* (a complex play, originally listed as a comedy) and *Cymbeline* (initially categorised as a tragedy).

The play has also been grouped chronologically with the other romances and categorised as one of 'last plays' or the 'late plays'. Shakespeare composed all of these plays during the final years of his life and, some critics suggest, as he was winding down to the end of his career. Indeed, Prospero's speech in Act IV scene 1, beginning 'Our revels now are ended' (148), has frequently been cited as a veiled reference by the playwright to his own imminent retirement. At the end of a long and prolific career, Shakespeare seems to be mellowing a little, eschewing the gruesome and nihilistic elements of some of his most compelling tragedies in favour of reconciliation and peace. His dramatic emphasis falls on the regenerative qualities of forgiveness, mercy and humility, which triumph over greed, pride, ambition and arrogance.

This emphasis on the resolution of generational conflict is clearly a running theme of the romances, as Shakespeare dramatises the handover of power and responsibility from one generation to the next. Having arranged the marriage between Miranda and Ferdinand, and in so doing secured the future of his family against the threat of chaos, Prospero is happy to abdicate his magical powers. Indeed, although all four plays contain dark elements which would be more suited to a tragedy, they all conclude 'happily'.

Common characteristics of the romances include Shakespeare's preoccupation with 'lost' children and the restoration of characters to their rightful positions in society. The revelation scene in *Pericles*, in which the eponymous hero is reunited

with his daughter, for example, bears comparison with that of Ferdinand and Alonso in Act V scene 1 of *The Tempest*. This theme of reconciliation and resurrection continues in *The Winter's Tale*; Hermione returns to life, having been cast as a statue for several years, while Perdita also makes a telling reappearance at the end of the play. The tempests and shipwrecks of *Pericles* provide a particularly useful analogue to *The Tempest*, not least because of their close links to thematic concerns like fate, providence, disorder and the smallness of man in the universal scheme of things. The risky nature of sea travel in Shakespeare's times made the ocean a **symbol** of man's impotence in the face of divine forces.

By focusing on themes such as resurrection, the mysteries and the power of the sea (an unpredictable and untamable force), Shakespeare also exhibits a desire to engage with more complicated stage effects. The Blackfriar's Theatre, which offered an indoor, lighted stage, was made available to the King's Men at this time, and this may therefore have provided a suitable incentive for Shakespeare to be more adventurous in his use of stage effects.

There are clearly striking similarities between Shakespeare's romances, though it would be unwise to generalise too much about their genesis. Aside from the general thematic similarities outlined above, the romances vary enormously in dramatic style. The action of *The Tempest*, for example, conforms to the unity of time, unfolding within a single afternoon. In contrast, *The Winter's Tale* takes place over a time scale of many years, with a 16-year gap at the start of Act IV, which is denoted by the appearance of Time as a chorus. When tackling issues surrounding genre, students should therefore be aware of the limitations of categorising a play too narrowly; *The Tempest* is at its most fascinating when its generic complexities are acknowledged and discussed rather than ignored or downplayed.

Play context

It is widely assumed that Shakespeare never left England, though the majority of his plays, in all genres, are set in other countries. Italy was particularly favoured because it was the origin of the **Renaissance** and home to many of the source texts which inspired Shakespeare and his contemporaries. Foreign settings also have the advantage of allowing comments on local political and social issues to be made circumspectly, as in *The Tempest*.

Shakespeare used known sources for 35 of his 37 plays, and it is assumed that the other two must have had sources as yet undiscovered. In this period, before, and for some time after (until the emergence of the aptly named 'novel' genre in the early eighteenth century in fact), originality of plot or character was not considered necessary or even desirable in literary works. A largely illiterate population and a traditional oral culture created a demand for the familiar and reassuring, as with children and their bedtime stories. Audiences already expected to know the basic storylines, settings and outcomes of plays they attended, and the skill and creativity of the playwright was demonstrated by the quality of the improvements made to an existing work, including the adaptation of the genre.

The Tempest differs from many of Shakespeare's plays in that it does not have a single major source. We know for certain that he made use of Ovid's *Metamorphoses* and Virgil's *Aeneid* for some scenes in the play, but there is also strong evidence that he drew on a number of pamphlets which described shipwreck and adventure in Virginia and the Bermudas, as well as William Strachey's 'A True Reportory of the Wracke and Redemption of Sir Thomas Gates, Knight' (first published 1625; written 1609–10) and Michel de Montaigne's 'Of the Canniballes' (1603; written 1578–80). Elements of plot and character may also have been borrowed from William Thomas's *History of Italy* (1549) and an array of other minor sources, such as the following:

- *Li Tre Satiri* from the *commedia dell'arte*
- William Thomas's *History of Italy*
- Ben Jonson's *Hymenaei, A Masque*
- Diego Ortuñes de Calahorra's *The Mirrour of Knighthood*

The printed text

No manuscripts of any of Shakespeare's plays have survived. Some of the plays were published during his lifetime, in editions known as 'Quarto' because of the size of the paper used. In 1623, after his death, a collected edition known as the First Folio was published, which contains all his plays except *Pericles*. Although the Folio is generally considered to be more reliable than the Quartos, the case for each play has to be assessed on its merits.

The Tempest was originally published in the Folio of 1623, having first been performed at court in 1611. No Quarto editions survive and there is therefore little debate about the validity of different textual variants. As this was the first play to be set in the Folio, it also appears that the compositors took special care to lay it down accurately, so it contains few textual **cruces**. There are, however, still one or two contestable issues with regard to the text. First, as the Arden editors discuss at length in their Introduction (pp. 124–38), the Folio edition was prepared by the legal scrivener Ralph Crane, who apparently performed some additional editorial procedures. He seems to have added a number of apostrophes to elide words where it might regularise the metre of the lines and to have interpolated stage directions that aid a reader's understanding of the text. These are, however, relatively minor changes, and the text of *The Tempest* is considered to be one of the 'cleanest' of Shakespeare's plays today.

Whichever edition of the play you use, a number of changes will have been made from the original text. Different editors are likely to have different views and to arrive at different conclusions in all these areas. The changes, and arguments for

them, are usually indicated in the textual notes, but the goal of an editor is generally to produce an edition which makes sense when acted on the stage, rather than to give an account of all the possible interpretations of the play.

The play on stage

The Tempest was first performed at court in 1611 and has enjoyed almost unbroken popularity ever since, though it has changed dramatically in form over the centuries. It has inspired operatic performances, film adaptations (such as *Forbidden Planet* (1956) and *Prospero's Books* (1991)), as well as mimes, poems (such as Percy Bysshe Shelley's 'With a Guitar, To Jane' and Robert Browning's 'Caliban upon Setebos'), and even a number of psychological, philosophical and sociological studies. This impressive list of literary offshoots serves to underline the fact that the play has always stimulated a vast array of different responses.

The Tempest is one of Shakespeare's shortest plays, but it is also one of his most dynamic and varied when performed. It is loaded with music and dances, masques and visual effects. The spectacular opening scene was a particular attraction to audiences of the seventeenth and eighteenth centuries, while its songs and musical interludes serve to increase its running time and to retain the audience's attention whenever the narrative drive of the play slows down. Indeed, after the initial drama of the first scene, the tempo of the play is not particularly fast. It has only nine scenes in total (excluding the Epilogue), four of which are in excess of 250 lines. Events, and the interaction of the characters, seem to flow more naturally than in some of Shakespeare's other plays, but the longer scenes can be a drain on the audience, and make it difficult to sustain dramatic tension. The fact that Prospero is entirely in control of all of the play's events from the moment the play starts also lessens this tension. Interest is therefore maintained through the two murderous sub-plots, the courtship of Ferdinand and Miranda, and our expectation of a revelatory **dénouement**.

Issues of race, gender and sexuality are all intrinsic to the meaning of *The Tempest*, and the interpretation of all of the most central characters has differed wildly as a result of casting choices. From initially being presented as a wronged duke and devoted father, Prospero's character has gone through a whole host of different interpretations. **Post-colonialist** readings of the play cast him as an empire-builder who sets out to appropriate a foreign land and 'civilise' its indigenous population (Caliban, Ariel). Where some directors have seen him as a caring and indulgent father, others have seen him as a despot and obsessive patriarch, whose voyeuristic interest in the marriage of his daughter has unpleasantly incestuous undertones. Still other directors have chosen to portray Prospero as a woman. Any actor playing the role of Prospero must have a sound awareness of these tensions in his character, and pay particular attention to facial expressions and body language during the telling scenes where he observes other characters without being seen himself.

The role of Prospero is an extremely demanding one, as he choreographs all of the play's events and speaks roughly one third of its lines. Even when he is not directly involved in the action, he is assumed to be aware of what is happening on other parts of the island, whether through Ariel's presence or by eavesdropping himself. Shakespeare's decision to conform to the unity of place also means that, if the stage is divided into different sections to represent the different parts of the island, some characters will remain on stage for long periods, having to stay in character even when they are not the main focus of the audience's attention.

Up until the nineteenth century the role of Caliban was invariably a fairly peripheral one, but he has perhaps been the focal point of twentieth-century productions of the play. He has been portrayed as a Native American, a South American and a black African, as well as a gay male character and, in Suniti Namjoshi's 'Snapshots of Caliban', a lesbian. In whatever form he has appeared, he has usually been a symbol of an oppressed minority of one kind or another. Contemporary debates about slavery, both before and after its abolition in the UK in 1838, informed directors' and critics' views of 'this thing of darkness' (V.1.275). Indeed, his appearance has historically been a major issue of contention. As discussed, he has had several ethnic incarnations, and certain references in the text suggest that he is more humanoid than human. Trinculo describes him as a 'deboshed fish' (III.2.25), and the several references to Caliban's fishiness in the play have led to the use of prosthetic scales and fins as part of his costume. He has also been played as a turtle in some productions. This combines his aquatic and earthy aspects and provides him with a shell under which he can hide at moments when he feels vulnerable to Prospero's magic, or the elements (in Act II scene 2, for example). Some directors have taken literally Trinculo's comment that Caliban is 'puppy-headed' (II.2.151–52), adorning him with a large pair of dogs' ears. In the wake of Darwin's theories of evolution, Caliban has also — in contradiction to all textual evidence — been played as an ape-like creature, representing an earlier evolutionary form of man.

Like that of Caliban, Miranda's role has altered dramatically since the play's first inception. In early performances her sharp outburst at Caliban in Act I scene 2 was reassigned to Prospero on the basis that the speech was rather too confident and unladylike to be suitable for her. However, the challenging and complex aspects of her character have subsequently been explored in much greater detail. An actress playing Miranda must decide how to balance her contrasting character traits, such as breaking her habit of exemplary obedience to her father's will by telling Ferdinand her name. Her innocence can be played as a great and noble virtue or tragic ignorance; she is perhaps naïve in declaring the likes of Antonio and Sebastian 'goodly creatures' at the close of the play (V.1.182), and her willingness to let Ferdinand cheat at chess, though a minor consideration in itself, suggests a worrying subservience on her part which could be transferred to other areas of her marriage.

Nevertheless, some critics argue that the chess match actually symbolises the equality and understanding between the young lovers as they begin their life together.

Ariel's relationship to Prospero is also open to a range of interpretations; he can be played as the 'malignant thing' (I.2.257) who grudgingly discharges his duties out of necessity, or as a willing assistant to Prospero, who shows genuine gratitude to the magician for ending Sycorax's magical imprisonment. At the end of Jonathan Miller's 1970 production Ariel repaired Prospero's broken staff as the magician's ship sailed into the distance, effectively appropriating the very powers which had been used to oppress him (see Arden Introduction, p. 114).

The Tempest has a large cast of relatively minor, or even absent, characters. We hear a lot about Sycorax and Claribel without them ever appearing on stage, while Alonso, Antonio, Sebastian, Gonzalo, Stephano and Trinculo play important roles in the development of the plot without ever stealing centre stage. The result of this is that the burden of dramatic tension shifts onto the more complex characters of Prospero, Caliban, Miranda and Ariel; it is on these pivotal roles that the success of a production invariably depends.

Critical history

In his 'Induction' to *Bartholomew Fair* (1614) Shakespeare's contemporary Ben Jonson implied that many successful plays of the time had achieved their popularity as a result of their fantastical plots or spectacular effects. He was bitter in his invective against '*Tales, Tempests*, and such like *Drolleries*', seemingly referring to Shakespeare's *The Winter's Tale* and, of course, *The Tempest*.

Such comments do more than simply illuminate Jonson's highly developed sense of competition. They also suggest that Shakespeare's romances had proved popular on stage, for whatever reason, and that slightly elliptical references like these would have been understood by a theatre-goer of the period.

Less than a century later the play was continuing to enjoy great popularity, and it received an extra injection of life as it was revised for the stage by two eminent playwrights of the time. In the 1669 preface to his and Davenant's 1667 adaptation of the play, entitled *The Tempest, or the Enchanted Island*, Dryden comments on the play's great success at the Blackfriar's Theatre earlier in the century. He and Davenant seemed keen to capitalise on this by adhering relatively closely to Shakespeare's text while also emphasising the complementary nature of some of the play's characters. Their rewrite involved the introduction of the parallel characters of Hippolito (a suitor who had never seen a woman before, in place of Ferdinand) and Sycorax (as Caliban's sister, not his mother), who provided foils for Miranda and Caliban. This made the play more **didactic**, emphasising its structural symmetry and strengthening its moral message. Dryden and Davenant's version also emphasised the difficulty of securing genuine repentance from villainous characters.

Even at the end of the play, as their boat sets sail for Europe, Antonio and Sebastian are seen plotting Prospero's overthrow once again.

It took around a century for the original text to be restored to the stage in the majority of productions. At this point a critical consensus seemed to reign over the character of Caliban, who tended to be interpreted as a straightforwardly evil character. However, this view began to be challenged more seriously as the nineteenth century went on, as commentators put Caliban's role into the context of growing unease over the global slave trade.

Few other plays have been reinvigorated with such success over a long period of time. The increasing importance of the character of Caliban in criticism of the play is one of the chief reasons for *The Tempest*'s longevity of appeal. He has provided a focal point for political and post-colonial readings of the play up to the present day. Although *The Tempest* was written at a relatively early stage in English colonisation of America and Africa, the political climate of several different eras and cultures has contributed a great deal to the various interpretations of Prospero's least willing slave. The magician's appropriation of the island likewise came under closer scrutiny as the issues of slavery and colonialism gained status on the political agenda. The global dominance of western European powers in particular sparked a range of different responses, as has the emergence of the USA as the world's only remaining superpower in the twenty-first century.

The debate about the factors that influence our intellect, morality and physical capabilities is also explored in the play, as Prospero bemoans Caliban as 'A devil, a born devil, on whose nature/Nurture can never stick' (IV.1.188–89). Although audiences of Shakespeare's day may well have agreed with this point of view, today's more tolerant and cosmopolitan viewers might question the morality of imposing one's own values on others and ask whether it is possible to judge any culture superior to another, rather than just different.

Current opinion about Prospero is still as divided as ever, though it leans slightly towards an uncharitable interpretation of his motives. Following the scientific works of **Freud**, and the **Oedipal** readings of *Hamlet* to which these gave rise, the purity of Prospero's relationship with Miranda has been called into question. In some productions, the tensions between Caliban, Prospero, Miranda and Ariel have also been manifested in various sexual relationships between the four characters.

The Tempest has received far more exposure on the exam specifications than either *Cymbeline* or *Pericles* (not least because of question marks over the authorship of the latter play), and has shared the limelight with *The Winter's Tale* as one of Shakespeare's most successful romances. It offers opportunities for more sophisticated analysis than any of his more conventional comedies, and has a tradition of producing a variety of alternative readings, which makes it a rewarding text to study.

A variety of critiques

Any play must be considered in relation to its historical and social background and the political climate which produced it, and be viewed in the context of contemporary attitudes, however unconsciously they are drawn on. On the other hand, our critical interpretations should include responses to the issues which concern us nowadays, such as the stereotyping of gender and race in the portrayal of women and different cultures from around the world. A **feminist** critique will try to ascertain whether the play challenges or accepts and endorses the patriarchal status quo and the misogyny of the time; a **post-colonial** critique will study the way Caliban is portrayed as the 'Other' in his own native land; **structuralist** approaches will look at language to expose the shifting and **ambivalent** relationship between words and meaning (signifier and signified); **post-structuralists** will look for what isn't there as well as what is, at how the plot is framed and at the assumptions being made. A combination of all of these critical approaches will produce essays which show an awareness of a range of reader responses and audience reactions, and which cover the examination assessment criteria.

Scene summaries and notes

Act I scene 1

A boat in the Mediterranean enters a tempest which threatens to sink it. The Boatswain challenges the storm to do its worst while warning his distinguished passengers, Alonso, Sebastian, Antonio, Ferdinand and Gonzalo, to stay in their cabins. The ship splits and Antonio and Sebastian desert Alonso, while Gonzalo resigns himself to fate and joins the king and Ferdinand in their prayers.

Despite being of noble lineage, most of the characters from Naples and Milan are described as cowardly in the face of the storm. Antonio and Sebastian are more concerned with self-preservation than loyalty. Although Antonio suggests 'Let's sink wi'th'King' (59), Sebastian responds with 'Let's take leave of him' (60). The two exit at this point, probably diving overboard. Gonzalo is introduced as a loyal and philosophical character, but he fails to see that rank means nothing in the throes of a storm. He tells the Boatswain to 'remember whom thou hast aboard' (19), but the Boatswain angrily retorts, 'None that I love more than myself' (20), highlighting nature's disregard for titles and noble birth. This sets the scene for an upsetting of the 'natural' order in which the ruling classes' prerogatives of power do not apply. The theme of destiny is introduced in Gonzalo's final lines as he exclaims, 'The wills above be done' (63). In retrospect this comment casts Prospero in a godlike role, as we later learn that he is controlling the storm.

Act I scene 2

Miranda watches from the shore as the ship is battered by the tempest, and asks her father to stop the storm he has conjured up. Prospero assures her that no one on the boat has been harmed. He then explains that he and Miranda landed on the island 12 years before, after Antonio's coup to depose him as Duke of Milan. We are told how the courtier Gonzalo provided them with water and food to survive the journey, along with Prospero's magic books.

Prospero sends Miranda to sleep and Ariel enters. The sprite describes how he tormented the ship's crew, before declaring that the boat is anchored in a quiet bay and that all those aboard reached shore safely. The rest of the fleet is heading back to Naples from Tunisia, assuming that their king is dead. Ariel then complains that Prospero has not yet set him free. Prospero reminds Ariel that he rescued him from imprisonment by the witch Sycorax (Caliban's mother). Prospero tells Ariel that he will be free in two days if he assists him. Ariel agrees, and exits to roam the island invisibly.

Miranda wakes and Caliban enters, cursing Prospero. We learn that Caliban used to roam the island freely before his master's arrival. Miranda taught him how to speak, but Caliban attempted to rape her, which is why he is now Prospero's slave. Caliban then exits to fetch fuel, under the threat of punishment from Prospero.

Ariel and his spirits enter, leading Ferdinand to Prospero's cave with a song. Seeing Ferdinand, Miranda immediately falls in love with him. Prospero privately congratulates himself on the success of his plan. Pretending to be suspicious of Ferdinand, Prospero then takes him captive. Miranda protests Ferdinand's innocence, but her father refuses to relent. The scene ends with Miranda comforting Ferdinand.

This is a crucial scene, which lays the foundations for the rest of the play and introduces several key themes. First, Prospero makes some of the longest speeches in Shakespearean drama as he tells Miranda (and the audience) of his usurpation, and their arrival on the island. By informing the audience about previous events, Shakespeare allows the play to conform to the unity of time; many key events have already taken place, and their consequences will be addressed during the action of the play. Prospero's admission that he spent much of his time as Duke of Milan 'rapt in secret studies' (77) also provides evidence that the coup against him was at least partially justified. The Florentine political philosopher Machiavelli argued that rulers should retain their power by shrewd judgement and ruthless action rather than by assertion of divine right — a precept of which the complacent Prospero was unfortunately ignorant.

The introduction of Ariel and Caliban raises the related themes of authority and slavery. Neither is entirely happy to help the sorcerer, and yet both are in thrall to his power. Despite being labelled a 'poisonous slave' (319), Caliban exhibits highly sophisticated

speech, expressing himself in beautiful, measured verse. This is in stark contrast to the rough prose of characters like Trinculo and Stephano whom we meet later, and raises the question of whether Caliban is the indisputably bestial character Prospero makes him out to be. His comment 'I am all the subjects that you have,/Which first was mine own king' (341–42) challenges the assumption that Prospero's rule of the island is legitimate, and draws striking parallels between Antonio's usurpation of the throne in Milan and Prospero's self-imposed rule of the island.

Prospero seems to be a dominant father who demands attention and obedience. While making his long speech to Miranda, he breaks off to demand 'Dost thou hear?' (106) and 'Dost thou attend me?' (78), even exclaiming 'Thou attend'st not!' (87) at one point. His desire to shape Miranda's life extends to her choice of husband, and he engineers her meeting with Ferdinand without her knowledge. Having allowed the relationship to start, he then enslaves Ferdinand as a form of love test, thereby asserting his indisputable power as the patriarch of the island.

The frequent references to fate, destiny, fortune and providence all contribute to a feeling that the lives of the characters are controlled by an outside force. Prospero claims to have landed on the island 'by providence divine' (59) and thanks 'bountiful fortune' (178) for bringing his enemies within his reach. He then asserts that the success of his plan depends 'upon/A most auspicious star' (181–82). All this shows humility before higher powers, but for the helpless and shipwrecked Italians it is Prospero himself who shapes their destiny. In conjuring the tempest he has harnessed the four elements (earth, air, fire and water) and now has total control of events on the island.

Act II scene 1

Alonso's group wander across the island, looking for Ferdinand. Gonzalo tells them to be cheerful about their miraculous escape from death instead of lamenting their losses. Adrian and Gonzalo then eulogise about the island, while Antonio and Sebastian mock their idealism. The conversation switches to the marriage of Alonso's daughter Claribel to the King of Tunis, from which the group were returning when they were shipwrecked. Alonso bewails the apparent death of Ferdinand, his heir, and his daughter's marriage, which means that she lives too far away from Naples for him to see her. Sebastian makes Alonso feel even worse by blaming him for permitting Claribel's marriage. Gonzalo chides Sebastian for being cruel, and embarks on a utopian speech in which he discusses what he would do if made King of this new island.

Ariel appears, and all but Alonso, Sebastian and Antonio fall asleep under his musical spell. Antonio then convinces Alonso to sleep, while he and Sebastian guard him. Instead, Antonio uses his time alone with Sebastian to persuade his companion to murder Alonso and usurp his throne. Having agreed to kill Alonso and Gonzalo between them, the two prepare to strike. However, Ariel appears, singing in Gonzalo's ear to wake him up. Sebastian pretends that he drew his sword to protect Alonso from wild beasts. Shaken by this, the king commands that the search for Ferdinand must go on, and the scene ends with the group moving on again.

The first of the play's sub-plots continues the theme of usurpation introduced in Act I scene 2. There is a clear parallel between Antonio's coup against his brother Prospero, Sebastian's pledge to murder his brother, and the plot devised by Caliban, Stephano and Trinculo against Prospero. On the island, natural order seems to have descended into chaos, and man's natural instinct for power and liberty inspires a series of murderous plans.

The reference to the marriage between Claribel and the King of Tunis allows Shakespeare to explore interracial relations, and acts as an interesting inversion of cultural stereotypes. Instead of dominating a 'primitive' foreign kingdom, as Prospero does, Alonso has effectively made his daughter — a 'fair soul' — the possession of a dark-skinned African. Although it is not clear why he agreed to the match, he may well have done so for political reasons, as a way of opening up trade routes between Europe and Africa. Sebastian's angry reaction to Claribel's nuptials certainly suggests that she did not marry for love. In plot terms, her distance from Naples means that she is now unlikely to succeed to her father's throne, and that Alonso would have no immediate heir if Ferdinand were to die, as all the characters assume he has done.

Gonzalo's utopian reflections derive from Michel de Montaigne's 'Of the Canniballes', a prose tract which considered the nature of humankind in the light of recent voyages to the New World. Montaigne argued that, contrary to the predominant belief of those conducting the explorations, the indigenous populations of foreign lands need not be considered culturally inferior to the European pioneers. Gonzalo seems to agree with Montaigne that 'civilisation' — or the development of concepts like trade, division of land and law — do not necessarily make man any better than living by more primitive or 'natural' laws. This philosophical speech echoes some of the concerns of the Boatswain in Act I scene 1, where we are reminded that all human beings are essentially made of the same matter and subject to the same natural dangers as one another, whether they are kings or servants, nobles or tribesmen. Gonzalo's philosophical considerations would have been particularly pertinent at a time when English colonies were being set up in the New World.

The barrage of contradictory adjectives used by the courtiers to describe the island tells us more about these characters than the play's setting. Whether the air breathes 'sweetly', or is 'rotten', whether the grass is 'lush and lusty' or brown and 'tawny', is less revealing than the fact that the loyal optimist Gonzalo sees the good in the island, whereas the cynical Sebastian and Antonio see only its faults. In this sense, the island itself has no definitive nature, and it is simply the respective evil or goodness of the characters which is reflected in their view of it. The quick wordplay between these characters also acts as light comic relief. It is full of trademark Shakespearean wit, which defuses the feelings of discomfort evoked in the last scene by Prospero's severe treatment of Ferdinand.

Act II scene 2

Caliban enters, collecting wood for Prospero and cursing his master. He sees Trinculo enter and, thinking Prospero has sent another of his spirits to torment him, Caliban hides himself under his 'gabardine'. Looking for shelter from another imminent storm, Trinculo spots Caliban and shares his cloak. Stephano enters, drunk and singing. In his inebriated state he mistakes Trinculo and Caliban for a four-legged creature. The mistake is soon discovered and the three drink together in celebration. Quickly getting drunk, Caliban promises to show Stephano the fertility of the island which he once revealed to Prospero. Stephano, assuming that he and Trinculo are the only survivors of the shipwreck, lays claim to sovereignty of the island. Singing for joy at his newfound 'freedom', Caliban leads his two new companions away.

The theme of art and illusion is further developed in this scene, as Caliban, Trinculo and then Stephano all misinterpret the visual data with which they are presented. Stephano's bottle of alcohol becomes central to these characters' perceptions, creating another alternative reality on the island and causing all three characters to lose their inhibitions. Stephano, and particularly Caliban, fantasise about their futures in a way that they probably would not if they were sober. Stephano explores his dream of becoming a king and Caliban hungers to be free of his enslavement to Prospero.

The language of the scene is infused with religious imagery. Caliban asks, 'Hast thou not dropped from heaven?' (134) and is told to swear his allegiance to Stephano 'by this bottle' (118) and (twice) to 'Kiss the book' (127, 139) — in other words the bottle, as if it were a holy text. Caliban's request 'I prithee, be my god' (146) could equally be directed at Stephano or at the bottle he holds. In this sense, alcohol becomes an alternative deity for the weaker characters to worship. It is an alternative source of power to Prospero's magic book, though its power is only temporary. By the end of the play, Caliban laments 'What a thrice-double ass/Was I to take this drunkard for a god,/And worship this dull fool!'(296–98).

The several references to Caliban's appearance add to the debate about what sort of costume an actor playing his role should wear. He is repeatedly referred to as a 'monster', is described as 'puppy-headed' (151–52), as a 'mooncalf' (105, 109), a 'cat' (82) and a 'devil' (87). Upon first seeing him, Trinculo asks whether he is 'A man or a fish?' (24–25) and exclaims that he is 'Legged like a man! And his fins like arms!' (32–33). As a man-fish, he unites the lower elements of water and earth, and is certainly no conventional man. For this reason both Stephano and Trinculo see the possible monetary value of bringing him back to Europe and presenting him to an emperor or charging the public to look at him. In the seventeenth century such 'freak shows' could prove very lucrative. Explorers of the New World brought back extraordinary breeds of animals and plants, and often made a healthy profit by exhibiting nature's curiosities to their countrymen when they returned home.

Act III scene 1

Ferdinand is carrying wood for Prospero while Miranda oversees his labours. Unaware that her father is watching, she offers to carry some of his load. Miranda then breaks her father's command by telling Ferdinand her name. They woo one another and — as Prospero looks on — agree to marry. They exchange fond farewells and Prospero speaks a short **soliloquy**, expressing his delight at the match.

This scene, like Act II scene 2, begins with the image of one of Prospero's captives collecting wood for him. Ferdinand's labours echo those of Caliban, and serve to draw an uncomfortable parallel between the two characters. Both are subject to Prospero's magical powers, and both obey his wishes against their will. Ferdinand, however, later falls into the magician's favour (unlike Caliban), thereby passing the love test which he has been set.

The language in this scene is in the register of courtly love, with Ferdinand and Miranda speaking in romantic **metaphors**, **superlative** constructions and **hyperbole** in order to express the depth of their love for one another. Ferdinand also emphasises the purity of his love for Miranda, asking permission to pray for her, and talking of his 'soul', Miranda's 'grace' and appealing to 'heaven' to witness his declaration of love for her.

Some critics argue that this scene of courtly romance is tainted with a sinister edge as Prospero watches his daughter select her husband. He obviously approves the match, and has engineered events so that the two meet in this way. In the seventeenth century it was usual for fathers to negotiate marriages for their daughters, but Prospero does so here while perpetuating the illusion that Miranda is allowed a free choice. She is unaware of his surveillance and offers her hand to Ferdinand without his permission. This is an image of female rebellion which might have made audiences uncomfortable were it not that Prospero is on stage to reassure them that Miranda is merely carrying out his will.

Act III scene 2

As self-appointed leader of his group, Stephano drunkenly appoints Caliban as his lieutenant or ensign. Trinculo gently mocks the pair and Stephano warns him that he will be hanged for mutiny. Ariel enters and, as Caliban details his sufferings at the hands of Prospero, mimics Trinculo's voice, shouting 'Thou liest' throughout Caliban's speech. Caliban asks Stephano to kill Prospero, and promises to serve him loyally if he does so. As Ariel's interventions increase in number, Stephano becomes violent, beating Trinculo. Caliban goes on to describe Miranda's beauty, and Stephano agrees to kill Prospero that afternoon in order to take the magician's daughter as his wife. The scene ends with Trinculo reconciled to the group and the three companions following Ariel's song off the stage once more.

The theme of authority is explored in more detail in this scene. Several characters who are accustomed to servitude devise a system of hierarchy between them. Stephano aspires to kingship, clearly looking to improve his lower-class position in an Italian court. Caliban

now seems to have forgotten his dream of once again becoming 'mine own king' and consents to becoming another man's subject in order to usurp Prospero. For many critics, he is a tragic figure who has forgotten how to enjoy independence, having been oppressed for so long. Trinculo mocks Stephano's vainglorious aspirations, but chooses to follow his orders after being promised the role of viceroy in the prospective new kingdom. Power and rank are factors which motivate human behaviour at all levels, and this comic sub-plot provides a pertinent analogue to the more sinister plots in the play. The comic element of this narrative strand is further emphasised through Ariel's invisible interjections and Stephano raining drunken blows on Trinculo, elements which would have added to the play's popular appeal.

The appearance of Ariel, who leads the characters off with his hypnotic songs at the end of almost every scene, implies that music is both a manifestation of Prospero's magic and an important agent of control in the play. As well as enlivening the performance, Ariel's musical talent lends the island a mysterious and dreamlike air, reminiscent of *A Midsummer Night's Dream* and the dream sequences in *The Taming of the Shrew*. This contributes to a continuing sense of confusion, both for the characters and the audience, as to what is real and what is imaginary.

Act III scene 3

Exhausted, Alonso and his group stop to rest. The disconsolate king accepts that Ferdinand is dead. Antonio and Sebastian secretly confer and plan to murder Alonso that evening. Prospero, invisible to the other characters, appears with his sprites, who bring in a banquet and invite the group to eat. As they approach, however, Ariel makes the banquet disappear. Alonso, Antonio and Sebastian draw their swords, but Ariel uses a charm which makes their weapons too heavy to hold upright. Ariel then informs the three men that they have been shipwrecked as a punishment for their usurpation of Prospero.

Stunned for a moment, Alonso determines to continue looking for Ferdinand, and to die next to him when he finds him. He exits, followed by Antonio and Sebastian, who resolve to fight the sprites if they appear again.

Although Prospero's magic has hitherto been used for benign purposes, the darker side of his art now becomes apparent. The scene is peppered with references to 'perdition', 'devils' and the 'fiend', all of which serve to highlight the potentially evil power of sorcery. At the same time, references to 'something holy' and the 'heavens' set up an opposing perception of magic as a force for good. Ariel's long speech, which he directs at the 'three men of sin', sees him assume the role of a godlike figure who, along with his 'ministers of fate', distributes justice to Prospero's persecutors. However, his actions are balanced on a knife-edge; though we can appreciate the justice of the way that Alonso, Antonio and Sebastian are being treated, Ariel — and Prospero too — is in danger of committing an act of **hubris** by assuming powers usually reserved for deities. As discussed on pp. 59–61, magic was considered evil in Jacobean times, in whatever form it appeared. Shakespeare therefore reminds us that, despite being portrayed as a 'good' character, Prospero can only return to his rightful place in society by renouncing his magic.

Act IV scene 1

Prospero addresses Ferdinand, explaining that he only treated him harshly in order to test his love for Miranda. Prospero then warns Ferdinand not to consummate the relationship until they are married, and Ferdinand agrees to this condition readily. Prospero then asks Ariel to organise a wedding masque for the young lovers. While the show is prepared, Prospero once again lectures Ferdinand on the importance of remaining chaste until he and Miranda are married. The spirits appear, and act out the masque, which is interrupted as Prospero remembers Caliban, Stephano and Trinculo's plot to kill him.

Ariel tells Prospero that he has charmed the three plotters, leading them through rough foliage and into a swamp. Pleased, Prospero commands Ariel to fetch his fine clothes and use them as bait with which to attract the plotters. Caliban, Stephano and Trinculo enter, sopping wet. Just as they are preparing to kill Prospero, Trinculo notices the magician's rich clothes. Despite Caliban's warnings, he and Stephano steal them; at this, Prospero sends his spirits after them in the shape of hunting hounds, and they exit, hurriedly pursued by the beasts.

Prospero praises his daughter richly, but states that even these compliments fall short in describing her merits. Miranda has been put on a pedestal as the ideal of feminine virtue, and Prospero continues to advertise her worth as if marketing a valuable asset, which, in a sense, she is. Prospero subsequently refers to his daughter as 'my gift, and thine own acquisition/Worthily purchased' (13–14), and yet there is also a strong sense that he has engineered the marriage for the benefit of the young lovers, and the future political stability between Milan and Naples.

The spirit masque is an example of a play-within-a-play — as in *A Midsummer Night's Dream*, *Hamlet* and several other works by Shakespeare — which serves the purpose of illuminating some of the play's wider issues. Its theme is closely related to Prospero's repeated injunctions to Ferdinand that he must not sleep with Miranda until they are married. It acts as a celebration of their union but also reiterates Prospero's pleas for pre-marital chastity, as is obvious in the sprites' desire 'that no bed-right shall be paid/Till Hymen's torch be lighted' (96–97), which closely echoes Prospero's own words in line 23 of the same scene. The masque also acts as a reminder that the play we are watching is itself a fiction, a theatrical illusion which must be examined for its symbolic value before it disappears. Once the show is finished, Prospero explains that this illusion is like life itself; both are transient and leave no trace behind once they are over.

The fact that Stephano lost his bottle (which was a symbol of his power) when Ariel led him into the swamp suggests that he is no longer in a position to command Caliban

and Trinculo. It presages the failure of his plot against Prospero and is a signal that the magician is preparing to reclaim his title as Duke of Milan. Stephano's self-destructive obsession with Prospero's rich clothes also underlines the danger of submitting to the desire for wealth and the vain trappings of power.

Act V scene 1

It is almost 6 o'clock and Prospero acknowledges that his plan is going perfectly. Ariel reveals that Alonso and his companions are charmed and trapped in a grove of trees. Prospero then traces a circle and states that he will relinquish his magic once he has completed one last rite. The captives are brought in, and Prospero frees them from his spell. He forgives Alonso and Sebastian for their crimes against him, though they are unaware of his presence. Prospero then dresses himself in his former style as Duke of Milan and commands Ariel to fetch the Boatswain, who has been charmed to sleep for the duration of the play.

The group now come to their senses. Alonso is not sure whether to believe his eyes, but he resigns his dukedom and begs forgiveness for his crimes. Prospero quietly warns Sebastian and Antonio that he knows of their plot to kill Alonso, but keeps their secret for the time being. Prospero sympathises as Alonso now bemoans the loss of his son. The magician states that he has lost his daughter in a similar way. At this news, Alonso exclaims that he wishes their children could both be alive to marry and rule Naples together. His wish is made true when Prospero opens the entrance to his cave and reveals Miranda and Ferdinand playing chess. Never having seen so many human beings before, Miranda is enchanted by the beauty of the assembled company.

Ariel enters with the Boatswain, who declares that Alonso's ship is fully repaired, despite the fact that it was badly split in the storm. Prospero then tells Ariel to set Caliban, Stephano and Trinculo free. Caliban, seeing Prospero restored to his ducal finery, fears punishment. Prospero acknowledges responsibility for his monster and commands him, Stephano and Trinculo to tidy his cell and return the clothes they stole. He then invites Alonso and his company to his cell for the night, where he will tell his life story. They plan to return to Naples the next day, where Miranda and Ferdinand will be married. This being done, Prospero can return to Milan and meditate on his death. Lastly, he fulfils his promise to Ariel, setting him free.

Despite the large number of entrances and exits in this scene, all the action is adroitly controlled by Prospero. He takes on his customary role as conductor of affairs, commanding Ariel to fetch characters, dispensing punishment to some and forgiving others. By authoring the fate of each of the protagonists, he assumes the part of the playwright, acting as a surrogate for Shakespeare himself. He is, once again, something of a god-figure, fulfilling Alonso's wish to see Ferdinand and Miranda married even as the king bewails the deaths of these two children. In a metaphorical sense he is opening graves and raising the dead, though he has promised to relinquish the magic which grants him this power. Sebastian accuses Prospero of being a satanic apparition, but Prospero's denial of the charge, and the magnanimity he shows in forgiving his brother, would have allayed the audience's fears about the nature of his magic.

Gonzalo is amazed at what has happened, and claims that the island has enabled all of the characters to learn a great deal about themselves. His statement characterises the play as a romance, in which a potential tragedy is averted by the characters learning from their sins, being rewarded by mercy, and determining to lead better lives in the future. Even Prospero goes on a journey of discovery, developing from a hard-hearted and vengeful man to a humble and high-minded individual. It should be pointed out, however, that it is Ariel who prompts him to show mercy at the end of the play, reminding Prospero of the importance of humanity. The sight of the magician weeping as he sees Gonzalo's tears reminds us of the play's moral message — that we must empathise with our fellow human beings and forgive the faults of others. Prospero himself acknowledges that the most admirable and exceptional action is to show forgiveness rather then vengefulness, arguing that, if his enemies are now penitent, he has no further reason to torment them.

Although the play has a dénouement of sorts, some critics argue that complete closure is not provided. Indeed, the future is uncertain for characters like Caliban, Antonio and Sebastian. It is unclear whether Caliban will be free to reclaim the island as his rightful home or will be shipped back to Europe to continue his servitude. Even Prospero's claim 'This thing of darkness I/Acknowledge mine' (275–76) is loaded with ambiguity. The magician may be admitting a fault in having ruled tyranically over Caliban, or in having tried to 'civilise' a creature who neither needed nor wanted 'civilisation'. On the other hand, as de facto ruler of the island, Prospero could merely be arguing that Caliban is a native islander, and therefore comes under his own jurisdiction regarding punishment.

Meanwhile, Antonio and Sebastian are by no means as repentant as Alonso, implying that Prospero may have been too hasty in renouncing the magic which protected him from their murderous plans. Nonetheless, Prospero's desire to return to Milan and reflect on his death suggests that he is at peace with himself and can now face death with equanimity. He probably does not have long to live, and has ensured that his dynasty will continue thanks to the events he has wrought on the island.

Epilogue

Having relinquished his magic, Prospero asks the audience to release him from their power by applauding him and blowing him home with their cheers. He asks them to forgive him for any faults in his performance, just as he has shown mercy to his own enemies.

The Epilogue is often cut by directors, but it serves an important function. The last distinction between illusion and reality is challenged as Prospero addresses the audience directly. Even in the play's final moments, there is a curious tension between what is

real and what is not; though Prospero acknowledges the audience's presence, he also wishes to be propelled back into the fictional world of the play. He is now an impotent character, unable even to secure his passage home without the help of the audience. This confers new power on those who have been watching the play, and highlights too that Shakespeare himself relies on the approval of the audience in order to survive as a playwright.

The Epilogue is the final bridge from the dream world of the stage to the reality of the audience. It forces the audience into a position of empathy in which they must exhibit the same mercy as Prospero himself has shown to the other characters, thus acknowledging and endorsing the moral message of the play.

Characters

Dramatis personae

Prospero

Prospero is the former Duke of Milan and a magician. Having been usurped from his throne by his brother, Antonio, he landed on the island 12 years before the action of the play. He is probably between 35 and 45 years old, though he is usually played as middle aged. He orchestrates the action of the play, exemplifying his mastery of the four elements (earth, air, fire and water) in the opening storm scene and controlling the other characters through his use of magical devices (often via the medium of Ariel). His name means 'flourishing' in Italian, and it is therefore fitting that he has regained his dukedom, acquired a son-in-law and brought the majority of his enemies to repentance for their evil actions by the end of the play.

Miranda

Miranda is Prospero's daughter, and arrived on the island with her father at the age of three. Her mother is referred to only once in the play, as 'a piece of virtue' (I.2.56). Miranda has no recollection of her, suggesting that she died either in childbirth or very early in Miranda's life. Miranda is now approximately 15 years old, and on the verge of womanhood. She has never seen any human apart from her father (and the humanoid Caliban). She shows compassion for the suffering of those aboard the tempest-tossed ships at the start of the play and is amazed by the beauty of the characters she meets in Act V. Having experienced so little of the world, Miranda also represents naivety; her name means 'wonder', which is apt, given her reaction to the new people she meets, and indeed others' reactions to her. At the end of the play she looks forward to the prospect of marriage to Ferdinand, which will take place when their ship reaches Naples.

Caliban

Caliban is the son of the witch Sycorax, who was pregnant with him when she was exiled from Algiers to the island by sailors who punished her for being pregnant out of wedlock. Caliban is roughly 24 years old, and his name is significantly close to an anagram of 'cannibal'. He is a native of the island and is probably dark-skinned, making him one of Shakespeare's three moors, along with Othello and Aaron in *Titus Andronicus*. He is symbolically linked to the elements of earth and water, and there are several references in the play which suggest that he shows some characteristics of a fish. Initially, he had a good relationship with Prospero and was adopted by him. However, after his attempted rape of Miranda, Prospero condemned him to a life of servitude. Whenever he disobeys his master, Caliban is plagued by sprites who pinch and torment him.

Ariel

Ariel is a sprite of the island. He was imprisoned in a pine tree for 12 years by the witch Sycorax before being freed by Prospero. He has served the magician ever since. Ariel is closely associated with the element of air, as he has the ability to fly and sings a number of songs in the play, which he uses to charm the human characters. Although his character is listed in the Folio with the female roles, Ariel is usually played as a male character, thus emphasising Miranda's isolation as the only woman on the island. Ariel complains about having to obey Prospero's commands at the start of the play, but works enthusiastically for his ends when motivated by the prospect of imminent release from servitude. At the end of the play Ariel is finally freed.

Alonso

Alonso is King of Naples and conspirator with Antonio in Prospero's usurpation. He lands on the island on the way back from his daughter Claribel's wedding to the King of Tunis. Alonso spends the play in a state of almost unbroken melancholy, bewailing the apparent death of his son and heir Ferdinand. At the end of the play he repents of his sins and gives up his throne, rejoicing in Ferdinand's survival and his betrothal to Miranda. He is a model of the character who is redeemed through his suffering, learning the error of his former ways.

Sebastian

Sebastian is Alonso's brother and a Neapolitan courtier. He is cynical in his pursuit of power, and is only thwarted by Prospero's magic when he attempts to murder Alonso for his crown. His relatively quiet presence in the final scene prompts doubts about whether or not he repents of his actions.

Antonio

Antonio is Prospero's brother, and the usurping Duke of Milan. He shows no remorse for his actions; on the contrary, he convinces Sebastian to murder Alonso

on the basis of his own success. Although Ferdinand mentions that Antonio has a 'brave son' (I.2.439) from whom he has been separated, we hear no more of this mysterious progeny throughout the rest of the play. He is virtually silent in the final scene, suggesting that he, like Sebastian, is not entirely sincere in his penitence.

Ferdinand

Ferdinand is Alonso's son and heir to the throne of Naples. He falls in love with Miranda at their first meeting, but is held captive by Prospero as a test of his love. For the duration of the play he believes his father Alonso to be dead, and finds a new family in Miranda and Prospero. He admires his future father-in-law's magic and shows his nobility by agreeing to practise sexual abstinence until he has married Miranda. Their wedding will take place when they arrive safely in Naples.

Gonzalo

Gonzalo is an old Neapolitan courtier and councillor, who was responsile for helping Prospero and Miranda survive at sea after their banishment. He represents the traditional virtues of the older generation (loyalty, idealism), in contrast to his younger companions, Sebastian and Antonio. He has an optimistic view of the island, describing it as a sort of utopia. Gonzalo's weeping at the end of the play prompts Prospero to cry in sympathy, and he is the only one of the courtiers who has no obvious reason to repent of his actions.

Stephano

Stephano is a dipsomaniac butler at Alonso's court. He is an ambitious and greedy man, who tries to take advantage of the apparent chaos on the island by making himself a king. He uses his bottle as a way of controlling Caliban and Trinculo, but is undone by his avarice when he attempts to steal Prospero's robes.

Trinculo

Trinculo is a Neapolitan jester who, like Stephano, sees the possibilities which a new social order on the island would offer him. Arguably he has more wit than Stephano but he nonetheless shares in the butler's drinking and ambitious plans to rule the island. He too is undone by the sight of Prospero's rich clothes, and is punished for his actions at the end of the play.

Prospero in charge

However he is interpreted, Prospero is at the heart of *The Tempest*'s meaning. He speaks roughly a third of the play's lines, and controls the plot with his magical powers and omniscient outlook. He is the central character of the play and our interpretation of it depends largely on how we view his interaction with the other characters. Some critics have argued that he is an allegorical figure who represents a European power which arrogantly colonises a foreign land, disrespecting its indigenous inhabitants and culture. Others think of him as a doting father whose main aim is to secure the safety and prosperity of Miranda in the future, despite being stranded on the island against his will.

Doting father?

Prospero's relationship with Miranda is a complex one. He expects unreserved loyalty from her, and is swift to reprove signs of disobedience in her character. When Ferdinand is captured and she dares to stand up for him, Prospero angrily retorts, 'What, I say,/My foot my tutor?' (I.2.469–70), implying that she is a dependent part of him who should not expect to overrule his judgement. Prospero claims to do 'nothing but in care' of Miranda, but he is politically astute in assuring his own safety along with his daughter's by marrying her to the heir of Naples. Some interpretations of the play also highlight the unpleasantly voyeuristic nature of Prospero's relationship with Miranda. It is unclear why he needs to listen in, unbeknownst to the young lovers, as they open their hearts to one another during the courtship scenes. Such an interest may well represent an unhealthy interest in his daughter's love life, and some directors have attributed Prospero with incestuous feelings towards her.

Prospero is an authoritarian character in many ways, and it is fortunate for Miranda that her desire to marry Ferdinand coincides with her father's wishes. It seems unlikely that her disobedience — for example in telling Ferdinand her name, despite Prospero's injunction against doing so — would be tolerated if she were to choose a different suitor. There is something a little sinister about the way the two young lovers are made to feel that their mutual love is a private and personal romance, when the audience is aware of Prospero engineering their meeting and then observing their courtship. Prospero has clearly given great thought to the match, as he uses Miranda as a bargaining tool. He refers to her as a 'gift' and an 'acquisition/Worthily purchased' (IV.1.13–14), and this mercantile language gives the relationship the unromantic aura of a business transaction. In many ways Prospero benefits from bringing up Miranda on an isolated island; he is able to mould her character to his will and create an environment in which he has an enormous influence over her choice of husband. It seems inconceivable that he would have accepted any dissent from her if she had preferred a different man for her husband. On the other hand, it could be argued that he deliberately arranged for her to meet a man to whom he knew she would be well suited.

Tyrant or teacher?

Caliban is often characterised as the native islander who is robbed of his rightful liberty and habitat by Prospero's appearance. There is, however, a lively debate to be had about whether Prospero treats Caliban unfairly or not. The magician's initial instinct is to teach him language and offer him shelter after his mother dies. It is only when Caliban abuses this care and attempts to rape Miranda that he becomes Prospero's enemy. However, the seeming charity of teaching him how to speak can

also be seen as a form of cultural imperialism — it is a skill which he has not needed before, and it furnishes him only with the ability to verbalise the new torments of his existence. As he exclaims to Miranda: 'You taught me language, and my profit on't/Is I know how to curse' (I.2.363–64).

Ariel, like Caliban, is Prospero's slave against his will. He, however, is careful to cultivate his master's good opinion in order to secure his freedom, knowing that it would be futile to oppose him. It is worth noting that Ariel seems at least to relish some aspects of his servitude (most notably when he teases the other characters invisibly), is thanked warmly by Prospero for his efforts and is eventually released, as promised, at the end of the play. He is also indebted to Prospero for his freedom, having been imprisoned by Sycorax's spell. In this sense Prospero is his saviour as well as his master.

Rightfully banished?

Prospero himself concedes that he was 'rapt in secret studies' (I.2.77) while Antonio plotted to replace him as Duke of Milan. Although this could be interpreted as showing how deceptive his brother was, Prospero implicitly acknowledges that he should have been concentrating his energies on matters of state rather than on the private pursuit of supernatural powers. He neglected his responsibility to his subjects, and was therefore partly culpable for his downfall. On the other hand, Prospero mentions to Miranda in Act I scene 2 that Alonso could not get away with executing him because of 'the love my dear people bore me' (141). It seems, then, that Prospero retained his popularity among the citizens of Milan, despite his slightly neglectful attitude to state affairs. Gonzalo's decision to furnish Prospero with supplies for his sea voyage certainly suggests that Prospero was a respected man who inspired loyalty and compassion in others.

Interestingly, it was widely believed at the time that, although usurpation was obviously undesirable, it was not beneficial to upset the balance of state once again by removing a pretender to the throne from power. Instead, subjects were expected to show loyalty to the new king — as in *King Henry IV*, parts 1 and 2 — in order to prevent further destabilisation of the commonwealth. In *The Tempest* this principle comes second to the notion that dishonesty must be punished, and the righteous ruler restored to his place in society.

Magnanimous magus

Shakespeare seems to have intended the play to end happily, with an aura of reconciliation. Prospero holds complete power over events on the island and is therefore the only character capable of bringing this about. Were he to hold on to his magic, he would seem suspicious to the audience, since it was his obsession with the supernatural which led to his usurpation in the first place; the fact that he does not want to make the same mistake again is highly significant.

There are, however, problems with the reactions of the other characters to Prospero's actions. In the whole of the scene Antonio says only one line, expressing his interest in the 'marketable' value of Caliban. He makes no explicit apology and shows no remorse for his actions. Sebastian is marginally more vocal, exclaiming, 'A most high miracle' (V.1.177) as Miranda and Ferdinand are revealed. However, he may well do so under duress, or with a heavy tone of irony, as he has just been caught by Prospero whispering that 'The devil speaks in him' (129). These two characters therefore seem to be anything but appeased by Prospero's actions; Dryden and Davenant's Restoration version of the play even includes a final scene whereby the two plot to attack Prospero on the journey home. Even Caliban, who expresses regret for his attempt to murder his master, is not contrite. He fears that he will be 'pinched to death' (276), and repents teaming up with a 'dull fool' (298), but tellingly never questions the morality of trying to kill Prospero. Alonso is undoubtedly repentant. He joins in with Gonzalo's expression of gratitude and wonder by calling 'amen' (204) and begging 'forgiveness' of Miranda (198) for trying to kill her. He is so grateful to find Ferdinand alive that he extends his love, gratitude and relief to the other characters.

It is possible to argue that Prospero's actions are noble, naïve, or both. It might be helpful to consider them in the light of political events in the real world. Do you, for example, think that countries like the USA and the UK would succeed in winning peace with other countries if they decided to give up their nuclear weapons? Or would it simply encourage their enemies to exploit this new weakness?

The 'god of small things'

The Jacobeans were familiar with the figure of the 'overreacher', a dramatic character who tries to attain powers beyond human limits and ends up suffering a downfall as a result. Prospero certainly attains powers well beyond the capabilities of most human beings, and in this sense he is an overreacher figure. His colonialist tendencies in ruling over the island's indigenous peoples (Caliban, Ariel and the sprites) also suggest that he has a desire to possess things which are not rightfully his. However, he is not a classic overreacher figure because he takes great pains not to show **hubris** in his actions. From as early as Act I scene 2 he thanks 'bountiful Fortune' (178) and 'Providence divine' (159) for all the luck he has had, showing humility for his survival, and for bringing his enemies to the island. Furthermore, he casts off his powers when they are at their strongest, indicating that he is aware of the responsibilities and dangers which go hand in hand with the abilities he possesses. A typical overreacher holds on to his/her powers until ultimately destroying him/herself. In this respect Prospero does not fulfil that definition, though he certainly exhibits some of the other characteristics of such a figure.

In Peter Greenaway's 1991 film *Prospero's Books* the character of Prospero writes the scenes as they take place, putting words into the mouths of the other characters.

He is unequivocally a godlike figure. He is **omniscient** and **omnipotent** within the boundaries of the island and nothing happens without his say-so. Indeed, *Prospero's Books* is merely emphasising the nature of the play's power structures, which may otherwise be overlooked. Everything on the island, from the natural rhythms of sleep to the direction in which characters walk round the island, is in Prospero's power. He even manipulates human emotions in the case of Miranda and Ferdinand, as their clandestine and emotionally charged meetings are in fact engineered and observed by him. The fact that Greenaway's Prospero speaks the vast majority of the play's lines also characterises him as a director or playwright, creating parts for all the characters on the island and making them behave in a way that he dictates. In this sense he is an incarnation of Shakespeare himself. Those scenes which emphasise Prospero's control over events (his confrontation with Ferdinand; the masque scene in Act IV; Act V, in which he assembles all the characters, and so on) hint at the playwright's level of control. A key scene, however, in which we gain a greater understanding of the gap between Prospero and Shakespeare, is the Epilogue.

A changed man

The Epilogue is the only scene in the play in which we see Prospero beg others for help. Bereft of his magic, he is at the mercy of the audience. It serves the purpose of showing him as a mere mortal who, stripped of his great power, is as vulnerable as the rest of us. We must therefore exhibit the same sort of mercy as he has just shown, indicating that we too have learnt to be magnanimous with our power. For some critics, this new Prospero inspires admiration and sympathy. For others, he is now an impotent tyrant who, without any method of self-defence, is in a position to be punished for the wrongs he has done to the other characters during the play.

Miranda, the lone woman

Women's parts in plays did not equal men's in number, size or status because they were written for boy actors with unbroken voices, since it was unacceptable for women to perform in public. However, Shakespeare was famously interested in female perspectives and psychology and women have significant roles in many of his plays.

Miranda's name means 'wonder' and Caliban describes her to Stephano and Trinculo as 'a nonpareil' (II.2.101), meaning that she has no equal. This is true in quite literal terms, as she is the only female character on the island. As a result, she becomes the focus for our study of gender issues in the play and a representative of female values in a patriarchal society. She plays a number of roles — as Prospero's doting daughter, as the object of Caliban and Stephano's lust, as Ferdinand's fiancée, and so on. However we view her role in the play, we must consider women's place in society at the time in order to understand her character.

Natural inferiority

According to the medieval chain of being, which was still given credence at this time, women came below men on the hierarchy of creation — and one rung above animals — since it was believed that they were of inferior intellect and moral understanding. It was unacceptable, therefore, for a woman to boss or overrule her husband or father (Eve's fault, and Lady Macbeth's). Women were expected to be seen but not heard, and to be obedient — which meant silent — even, or especially, in their husband's or father's presence. Miranda has very few lines, and is repeatedly told by Prospero that she must listen intently to his tale in Act I scene 2. Miranda is, however, different from the typical woman of her times in so far as she was brought up away from the constraints of society. She is generally obedient to Prospero, but is nonetheless spirited in her attitude to Caliban, calling him an 'Abhorrèd slave' (I.2.351). She has at least the appearance of autonomy in her choice of husband, and is not afraid to get engaged to Ferdinand without her father's permission; she doesn't realise that he has planned their meeting all along. Indeed, it is crucial that the illusion of Miranda's freedom is just that; she would almost certainly be subject to the same constraints as other women of her time if she ever dared go against Prospero's wishes.

Daddy's girl?

In many ways Miranda conforms to the patriarchal ideal of the woman who obeys male authority. She admits that, having spent the vast majority of her life on the island, 'I do not know/One of my sex' (III.1.48–49), and therefore judges her own values of womanhood according to what she has been taught by Prospero. She is self-deprecating, doing her best to please others and apologising for trouble she causes. For example, during her father's long speech in Act I scene 2 she apologises for being a burden to him when they were set adrift at sea, exclaiming: 'Alack, what trouble/Was I then to you!' (I.2.151–52). She is compassionate too, watching the ship wracked by the tempest at the start of the play and wailing: 'O I have suffered/With those that I saw suffer!' (I.2.5–6). She is aware of the importance a patriarchal society places on female chastity, emphasising her own 'modesty' when Ferdinand compliments her as a 'wonder', and answering: 'No wonder, sir,/But certainly a maid' (I.2.428–29). She also acknowledges the importance of showing subservience to men, telling Ferdinand: 'I'll be your servant/Whether you will or no' (III.1.85–86), and deciding that 'I have no ambition to see a goodlier man' (III.1.484) within hours of first meeting him. Overall, Miranda shows that she is aware that her chief asset is her 'plain and holy innocence' (III.1.82), and takes great pride in her trusting and dutiful character.

She does, however, proceed in her engagement to Ferdinand without seeking her father's approval, and she disobeys him by telling Ferdinand her name. When she attempts to defend him against her father's wrath, Prospero angrily barks, 'What, I say,/My foot my tutor? (I.2.469–70), making explicit the fact that he does

not expect his will to be opposed in any way. Prospero also shows concern that Miranda will not be able to resist sexual temptation, as he twice warns Ferdinand not to consummate his relationship with her until they are legally married. Furthermore, her outburst at Caliban in Act I scene 2 shows that she is a woman of some spirit when she is wronged. Her harsh invective is hardly the sort of language one would expect from a shy and retiring member of the nobility.

A valuable commodity

Literally a 'nonpareil', Miranda has no peers on the island and therefore becomes the focus of male sexual attention by default. It is Caliban's lust for her which sparks the great animosity between master and servant, as he attempts to rape her — perhaps as a way of overturning the hierarchy which makes her his teacher, and therefore his superior. Caliban later uses her as a political tool, using her beauty as a way of convincing Stephano that he should murder Prospero and take over the island, with Miranda as his queen. This offer exemplifies the male desire to possess female beauty, using it as a way of expressing status.

Ferdinand worships her (as she does him), calling her 'So perfect and so peerless' (III.1.47). Alonso thinks she is a 'goddess' when she is revealed in Act V scene 1, contributing to the sense that she is an angelic or ethereal creature. Prospero too heaps eulogies on her, calling her a 'cherubin' in Act I scene 2 (152) and claiming in Act IV scene 1 that 'she will outstrip all praise,/And make it halt behind her' (20–21). These terms of praise border on the idolatrous, creating an image of female perfection. This is, however, potentially dangerous, as any woman who is seen as divine runs the risk of disappointing her worshippers. Prospero also sees the potential advantages of having such a sought-after woman as his daughter. He is able to use her sexual appeal as a bargaining tool to secure his and her future safety. By marrying her to the prince of Naples he doubles his own political influence and dissolves the animosity between Milan and Naples which led to his own usurpation.

The fact that Miranda is the only woman on the island has further implications for her relationship with Prospero. There are parallels between their relationship and that of the main characters in the Marquis de Sade's story *Incest*. In that tale a controlling father educates his daughter away from the rest of society, making her utterly dependent on his view of the world. He then goes on to seduce her. Although there is no explicit sexual tension between Prospero and Miranda, some critics have suggested the possibility of this kind of reading, particularly given the secretive nature of Prospero's involvement in her engagement to Ferdinand.

Absent women

Although we hear of her malevolence, imprisoning Ariel and issuing 'earthy and abhorred commands' (I.2.273), Sycorax never appears on stage, having died before the action of the play. She is called a 'witch', a term often reserved for women who exhibited masculine characteristics, ugliness or alleged sexual congress with the devil (as in *Macbeth*). The last of these characteristics is particularly important, given that Sycorax gives birth to the 'devil' Caliban. In some ways Sycorax is not considered as a 'real' woman; she exhibits 'male' traits of subversiveness and cruelty, harnessing her magic for unnatural ends. Perhaps her most important role is to represent 'bad' or 'black' magic, therefore providing a foil to Prospero and emphasising the benign nature of his own powers.

Miranda's mother is mentioned only once, and is termed 'a piece of virtue' by Prospero. In other words, her goodness equates to sexual fidelity. We are told that he believes Miranda is his daughter because his wife was so faithful, and she is held up as an example of fine womanhood.

Claribel provides an interesting foil to Miranda, being another 'lost' child in the play, and Ferdinand's sister. Alonso married her to the King of Tunis for political advantage, thus providing a parallel to Prospero's own political machinations in pairing Miranda with Ferdinand. Claribel's predicament also serves to highlight the difficulty of being an obedient woman at the time; Sebastian claims that, in marrying her husband, she 'Weighed between loathness and obedience at/ Which end o'th'beam should bow' (II.1.132–33), unable to quell her repulsion from Tunis but likewise unwilling to disobey her father.

Caliban: 'this thing of darkness'

Despite speaking under 200 lines in *The Tempest*, Caliban is, for many critics, absolutely central to the way the play is interpreted. He is a powerful and **emotive** symbol of social 'otherness', whether he is considered as a primitive monster or a 'noble savage'. He is crucial to our understanding of the play's ideas and characters because so many different interpretations depend on Caliban's interaction with his habitat and the people around him. It is possible to sustain almost diametrically opposed opinions of him while providing strong textual evidence for either point of view. He can be interpreted as an ungrateful wretch with no appreciation of the charity he received at Prospero's hands, or a well-meaning creature who is unable or unwilling to accept a foreign ideal of 'civilisation'. It is also debatable whether he is right to claim ownership of the island. His decision to embrace further servitude by succumbing to the charms of Stephano and his liquor contributes yet further troubling and compelling material to the debate. Each student must engage with just these sorts of complexities in order to enjoy a rewarding study of Caliban's character, and of the play.

'Something fishy'

Caliban's appearance is still a matter of some debate in the critical community. Over the centuries he has been played as a Native American, a black African and any number of humanoid/animal hybrids.

The most frequent references to his appearance, however, are fish-related. When Trinculo first stumbles across him in Act II scene 2 he asks: 'What have we here, a man or a fish?' (24), before settling on the evaluation that he is 'A strange fish!' (27). In Act III scene 2 he goes on to call him a 'deboshed fish' (25) and Antonio weighs in at the end of the play, calling him 'a plain fish' (V.1.266). The term 'puppy-headed' (II.2.151–52), meaning stupid, should probably be read metaphorically, though some productions have cast him as a doglike creature on the basis of this quotation. The word 'monster' is frequently applied to Caliban, suggesting that he is some sort of unnatural being. He is called a 'savage and deformed slave' in the cast list, a 'misshapen knave' by Prospero (V.1.268) and a 'mooncalf' (meaning someone who is born deformed) by Stephano on several occasions. In Jacobean times it was believed that unnatural birth or deformity were outer manifestations of an evil soul, hence women with warts or other physical impairments were often targeted as witches.

In terms of race, Caliban is almost certainly dark-skinned, though his exact ethnic background is difficult to ascertain. He was probably conceived in Algiers, suggesting he is of African origin, and is described as a 'freckled whelp' by Prospero (I.2.283). Stephano, in his first, drunken glimpse of Caliban under his gaberdine in Act II scene 2, thinks he sees 'savages and men of Ind', which could refer to East or West Indian peoples (57). The tag of 'devil' or demi-devil' is also applied to him several times, and comes with the implication that Satan was represented by blackness. Prospero's assertion that he is a 'thing of darkness' (V.1.275) can therefore be read as literal, metaphorical, or both.

Caliban's past

Caliban lived alone on the island before Prospero's arrival, and there are several references in the play to this period of independence. From the conversation between Ariel and Prospero in Act I scene 2 we know that Caliban was born when Sycorax arrived on the island and Ariel was imprisoned by Sycorax for 12 years, until Prospero came and broke her spell. It is now 12 years since Prospero's arrival, so Caliban is probably around 24 years old. In that period he has changed from being a trusted and cared-for companion to an outcast, confined to his cell and threatened with cramps and stitches whenever he disobeys Prospero. There is evidence of a strong relationship between him and Prospero at one point; Caliban remembers how the magician 'strok'st me, and made much of me' (333) when he first arrived, and he revealed 'all the qualities o'th'isle' to him in return (337). Miranda claims she 'pitied' him, as a brutish creature unable to speak (353). Prospero too says that he showed Caliban 'human care' until he attempted to rape Miranda (346). It is certainly very difficult to establish who is most at fault for the current diplomatic disaster between the two sides. Some critics argue that teaching Caliban the ways of human beings was itself an act of cruelty. By attempting to civilise an inherently bestial creature, Prospero and Miranda have turned natural instincts — for example that of procreation — into shameful and corrupt acts, much as Adam and Eve's innocence turned to lasciviousness when they tasted the apple of knowledge in Eden. On the other hand, Caliban can be interpreted as an agent of evil, who repaid the charity he received with betrayal of the worst kind.

Changing perspectives

When *The Tempest* was first performed, critics described Caliban as a demonic figure of the kind he is painted as by most of the other characters. Early interpretations of his character were inseparable from the issue of race. If he is played as Shakespeare's third and final Moor (after Othello and Aaron in *Titus Andronicus*) it is unsurprising to find that early audiences were hostile to him, given the relative racial intolerance at the time. It is significant too that his principal crime (the attempted rape of Miranda) is one of lust; the familiar stereotype at the time of black men as virile and lascivious is also played on heavily in *Othello*. The radical change in opinion surrounding the character of Caliban is therefore intrinsically linked to the racial and political sympathies of the cultures in which *The Tempest* has been performed over the years.

The changing political climate has certainly shaped views of Caliban. The collapse of slavery brought about an evolution in racial attitudes which encouraged more positive interpretations of his character. The play has also been transplanted into a number of settings in which Caliban represents a repressed minority other than a racial kind. It seems that, regardless of his colour, creed or nationality, Caliban has become a symbol of victimisation in the face of imperialist forces. As global knowledge about indigenous cultures has grown, and the tenets of relativism have become more widely accepted, Caliban has grown in stature as a character, fuelling a huge body of critical work.

'Mine own king'?

At the end of the play Prospero intends to return to Italy; it is unclear what will happen to Caliban, however. He expresses no wish to travel to Europe, and indeed only wants to regain possession of 'his' island. However, he is still in thrall to Prospero, and it is possible that he might be transported back to Italy as a slave. Almost as soon as he meets Caliban, Trinculo notes that he could be a profitable attraction if brought to England, and Stephano also perceives him as an exotic gift, worthy of 'any emperor' (II.2.69). This theme is emphasised in one of Antonio's few comments in Act V, when he calls Caliban 'a plain fish, and no doubt marketable' (V.1.266). It was common practice for travellers to bring back evidence of their journeys to corroborate their outlandish stories, and Caliban may well end up as the victim of just such a trend after the action of the play is over. This seems particularly likely in the light of Prospero's final statement of ownership: 'This thing of darkness I/Acknowledge mine' (V.1.275–76).

Even if Caliban were to be set free on the island, his fate would be uncertain. He has been partially 'civilised' by Prospero and Miranda, and it is doubtful that he would be able to return to his original state after they had gone. Having been forced into servitude for so long, it is debatable whether he even knows how to be free, as exemplified by his decision to trade in his enslavement with Prospero in favour of becoming Stephano's inferior in Act II. Given that Caliban's mother was responsible for imprisoning Ariel for 12 years, it is also unclear how his relationship with the sprites on the island would develop after Prospero's departure. Ariel is still in possession of magical powers, and it is not altogether fanciful to imagine him as next in the line of masters ruling over Caliban, as Jonathan Miller's production suggests (see Arden Introduction, p. 114).

Caliban's poetry

Caliban speaks in evocative and beautiful verse, which is as advanced and complex as that of any character on the island. This is particularly apparent in his mystical description of how 'the isle is full of noises' (III.2.136), and in the terrifyingly eloquent curses he directs at Prospero. His encounters with the bawdy and abrasive characters of Stephano and Trinculo bring out the poetry of his language, and his superior intellect; where they are seduced by the ornate trappings of Prospero's robes in Act IV, Caliban sees them for the worthless 'trash' (224) that they are.

There is no doubting Caliban's expressive capabilities. However, the language he has been taught is also a tool of cultural imperialism; for all the complaints and oaths he throws out, he can only express himself within the bounds of what others have taught him. It is a curious paradox that Caliban was neither able, nor ever had any reason, to curse until Prospero came along and furnished him with both the ability and the motivation for so doing.

The tempest

Travelling by sea in Shakespeare's day was much more dangerous than it is today, and most people were unable to swim, so if a boat split it was very unlikely that there would be many survivors, let alone that all of the crew would survive. It therefore seems miraculous that in *The Tempest* the Italian courtiers and crew survive the storm.

Storms or disturbances in nature — as we see in *King Lear* and *Macbeth*, among other Shakespearean plays — were often considered to be portents from the gods which showed their divine dissatisfaction with earthly events. Indeed, Ferdinand sees the storm as some sort of supernatural intervention. Ariel describes in Act I scene 2 how the king's son cried out: 'Hell is empty,/And all the devils are here!' (214–15) as he leapt overboard.

Staging

The tempest scene at the start of the play raises a number of issues concerning staging. It is possible to dramatise well with budgets of varying sizes, whether through the use of expensive pyrotechnics or a simple blacked-out stage, sound effects and strobe lighting. Regardless, it remains an appealing spectacle which would no doubt have been a significant attraction to audiences of Shakespeare's day. The limited stage technology available in Jacobean times meant that the tempest was probably represented largely by drums or other percussion instruments which would create a 'wall of sound' effect, allowing the audience to imagine the physical presence of the towering waves and blazing masts. Fireworks or torches may also have been used to represent the pyrotechnical aspect of the storm. Nowadays, theatrical effects of this kind can be reproduced more convincingly (and more safely) if a sizeable budget is available to a director. Perhaps most important of all has been the advent of video technology. Some directors choose to project footage of the storm onto a screen at the back of the stage before the action on the island commences. This technology also accounts for the success of film adaptations of the play, such as *Prospero's Books* (1991), which used the medium of film as a way of side-stepping many of the problems endemic in a stage production of the play.

Significance of the tempest

Dictionary definitions of the word 'tempest' are 'A violent windstorm, frequently accompanied by rain, snow, or hail' or 'Furious agitation, commotion, or tumult; an uproar'. This second definition is most useful because it suggests that Shakespeare wanted to emphasise the impression of temporary disorder brought about by the unnatural usurpation of Prospero. The word suggests emotional disturbance too, and is linked to the descriptive word 'tempestuous', which is often attached to people whose emotions vary wildly; in *King Lear*, for example, Lear is so distraught by the betrayal of his daughters that he exclaims in Act III Scene 4: 'The tempest in my mind/Doth from my senses take all feeling'. Such feelings are, however, transient by definition, since emotions — like the weather — are subject to change and are never entirely constant.

The sense of disorder engendered by the word 'tempest' reflects Shakespeare's preoccupation in the play with the conflict between chaotic, unpredictable events or behaviour and the imposition of order and temperance (self-restraint) upon them. This is a key theme in the play; man must not simply follow his base desires (like Caliban, or indeed the usurpers), but must impose reason and morality in order to resist corruption.

Symbolism

The stormy seas can be seen to represent the current state of chaos in the world. The established order has been overthrown by the 'unnatural' usurpation of the

duke Prospero by his brother Antonio. The elements seem to represent this imbalance. It is also pertinent that the elements do not judge a man by his rank. When the nobles come out on deck to see what is happening, they do not serve to calm the situation. They simply get in the way of the crew, who are doing their best to save the ship. Referring to the waves, the Boatswain asks: 'What cares these roarers for the name of king?' (I.1.16–17). Indeed, all men are equal before the might of nature.

As we learn later, Prospero is commanding the storm. In this sense it can be interpreted as representing his anger and thirst for revenge. Just as King Lear's mental turmoil is manifested in the wild storms which rage on the heath in his madness, so this tempest shows Prospero's wrath being visited on his enemies. This is an example of the literary device of **pathetic fallacy**. By the end of the play the storm is over; Prospero has been restored to his rightful place in society and this equilibrium is represented by the 'calm seas' and 'auspicious gales' which the magician promises for the Europeans' homeward voyage in Act V scene 1 (315).

Prospero's role as commander of the storms also suggests that he is something of an omnipotent or godlike figure, who has the power to control forces usually beyond human influence.

Emergency exits

As the storm rages and death for all the characters appears imminent, we are given some clear hints as to their true personalities. At first Antonio shows loyalty to Alonso, shouting 'Let's all sink wi'th'King' (59), but this noble sentiment is soon outweighed by the desire for self-preservation and he exits hurriedly with Sebastian, responding to the latter's suggestion: 'Let's take leave of him' (60). The fickleness shown by both characters emphasises how selfish they are and foreshadows their scheme to murder Alonso and Gonzalo in Act II scene 1. In contrast, Gonzalo is much more philosophical in the face of death. He is dignified, hoping that he will survive but resigning himself to fate, saying: 'The wills above be done' (63). Ferdinand and Alonso are below deck, at prayer. This supports an interpretation suggested by the rest of the play, that Ferdinand is a pious character. It does, however, make our understanding of Alonso more complex. His penitence at the end of the play appears more convincing in the light of the suggestion that he is a religious man, and also implies that he may already have repented privately for the wrongs that he has perpetrated against Prospero.

Why *The Tempest*?

Shakespeare tended to favour **eponymous** titles for his plays, so it is something of a puzzle that he chose to call this piece *The Tempest* instead of *Prospero*, *Prospero's Island* or something similar. However, those plays which have eponymous titles tend to be tragedies or histories, where the action is focused almost entirely on the central character's progress towards his fate (*Hamlet, Othello, King Lear, Macbeth, Richard III*, for example). Although Prospero is undoubtedly at the centre of the play's action, the audience's attention is focused on the changes which are brought about in other characters as a result of events influenced by him. In this sense he is the agent for change in the play rather than its focal point. Indeed, at the end of the play it is less important that Prospero regains his dukedom than that his daughter is now united with his erstwhile enemy's son, thus reducing the likelihood of another coup. The fate of Prospero takes second place to the restoration of a general sense of happiness and equilibrium. Both the words 'tempest' and 'temporary' are etymologically linked to the Latin word *tempus*, meaning 'time', suggesting that the play takes place under transient conditions: the audience and the characters are experiencing a temporary state of elemental discord which is out of the ordinary and will therefore be resolved. Given that the play is characterised as a comedy in the Folio of 1623, and that it has a loosely 'happy' ending, the audience would have expected the initial disorder and confusion of Act I to give way to resolution and peace at its end.

The island

The island on which Prospero and Miranda were wrecked has been carefully crafted by Shakespeare to reveal a great deal about his characters. Its location, its inhabitants and its natural properties all influence our understanding of the play and its themes. It is very important to understand why Shakespeare chose to set the play on the island, and to be able to discuss its symbolic significance as well as the more direct, physical, consequences the setting has on the plot.

Where in the world?

Although the exact location of the island is unspecified, we know from Ariel's reference in I.2.234 that it is in the Mediterranean. Lampedusa and Pantelleria are two of the most likely locations for the island. Several others in the same waters have also been suggested, including Jalitah. Alonso and his courtiers would have left from Naples, in the south of Italy, arriving in Tunis for the wedding of Claribel. It is on their return that they are hit by the tempest and washed up on Prospero's island. As the Arden edition indicates (see Introduction, pp. 48–49), the island is probably close to the African coast, since Caliban's mother was exiled there from Algiers. This allows us to deduce that the 'freckled' Caliban is most likely of African origin himself. Knowledge of his probable skin colour is important to our understanding of how other characters, and the audience, would have responded to him, particularly given the presence of a thriving slave trade in Europe at this time.

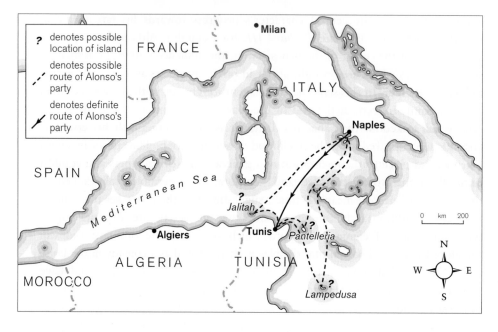

The island's resources

The island has many aspects and is neither totally benign nor entirely inhospitable. The way the characters respond to it therefore tells us a great deal about them. For example, in Act V scene 1 Ariel describes the 'line-grove' (a group of linden trees) which defends Prospero's cave from the elements (10). However, Alonso and his party have only experienced it as a prison, having been kept there until Prospero decides to break the spell that has been cast on them. There is also a clear disparity between the view of the island held by Gonzalo and Adrian on the one hand, and that of Sebastian and Antonio on the other. Where Gonzalo praises the island's grass as being 'lush and lusty' (II.1.55), Antonio calls it 'tawny' (57). Adrian asserts that 'The air breathes upon us here most sweetly' (49), but Sebastian responds with the jibe: 'As if it had lungs, and rotten ones' (50). The different reactions of these pairs of characters allow us to juxtapose the **utopian** viewpoint of Adrian and Gonzalo with the cynical, **dystopian** perspective of Antonio and Sebastian. It is no surprise to find that the first pair are loyal and optimistic in their service of Alonso while the latter are deceitful plotters against his life.

Caliban, who has grown up on the island and therefore knows it well, initially offers to show Prospero 'all the qualities o'th'isle,/The fresh springs, brine-pits, barren place and fertile' (I.2.337–38). This quotation hints that there is both a productive (or 'fertile') side to the island and a less hospitable (or 'barren') one. Once Caliban feels that his treatment at the sorcerer's hands has been unfair, he is quick to emphasise the potential evil on the island, calling up 'infections…/From bogs, fens, flats' against Prospero (II.2.1–2). However, this does not stop him from trying to ingratiate himself with his next ruler, Stephano, by the same means he used to befriend Prospero. In Act II scene 2 he indicates that he knows where to 'pluck…berries' (157), where to find 'fish' and 'wood' for fires (158). He goes on to assert that he knows 'where crabs grow' (164), where to find 'a jay's nest' (166) and dig for 'pignuts' (165), how to catch a 'marmoset' (167) and where to find 'clust'ring filberts' (168) and 'Young scamels' (169). This rich array of references indicates that the island has a great deal to offer if one is in tune with its secrets — as Caliban undoubtedly is. In stark contrast, Ariel describes how he leads Caliban and his newfound companions 'through/Toothed briars/sharp furzes, pricking goss, and thorns' (IV.1.179–80) before leaving them 'I'th'filthy mantled pool' near Prospero's cell in Act IV scene 1 (182). The island can therefore be seen both as an Edenic paradise, full of natural beauty and bounty, or as a wild and untamed location, against which the human characters must fight in order to achieve their aims.

Importance of the location

In dramatic terms, the great distance between Italy and the island makes Prospero and Miranda's survival seem miraculous. Bearing in mind that they travelled on 'A rotten carcass of a butt' without a sail (I.2.145), it is hardly surprising that Alonso, Antonio et al. are amazed to find the usurped Duke of Milan alive and well 12 years later. Despite highlighting how incredible their survival is, this distance also serves to show that Prospero's power has its limits, since he has been unable to find his way home with his magic up to now. The distance gives the island an aura of exoticness or 'otherness' which allows us to **suspend our disbelief** more easily when watching the fantastic spectacles of the play on stage.

The fact that the island is relatively inaccessible to the outside world also means that it becomes a **microcosm**. In much the same way as William Golding used an island setting in *Lord of the Flies* to explore the philosophical and moral conundrums of the twentieth century, Shakespeare's use of the island allows us to reflect on the true nature of man outside the boundaries of a familiar society. The innocent Miranda has certainly benefited from being cloistered away from a corrupt society, in that she shows compassion and love for her fellow humans. However, in Act V scene 1 she hastily calls the assembled group of characters 'goodly creatures' before she has had time to differentiate between the relative virtues of, for example, Gonzalo and Antonio.

The island setting also allows Shakespeare to explore the ambitious nature of man in great detail. Stephano aspires to being King of the island despite thinking that there are only five humans on it (one of whom — Prospero — he is planning to kill). He asserts his newfound authority over Caliban and, to a lesser extent, Trinculo, as soon as he has the opportunity to do so, appointing himself as their leader on the basis that he has a bottle of liquor. Even the noble Gonzalo hypoth-

esises about the exciting possibilities of running a classless state, of which he would, paradoxically, be king. It seems, then, that Shakespeare is suggesting that the desire to rule — or be ruled — is innate in human beings. Caliban, having once been his own master, as he remarks in Act I scene 2 (343), has been taught to be subservient and, in some respects, now seems unable to act independently. Instead he relies on the help of others to execute his plot against Prospero.

The island can therefore be seen as a philosophical space in which Shakespeare explores the issues of his day, as well as shedding light on moral and intellectual problems which continue to puzzle us today.

Unity of time

The three **unities** of place, action and time, were originally described by Aristotle in his *Poetics*. He considered them to be three factors which influenced whether or not a play appeared realistic to its audience. *The Tempest* conforms to the unity of place because all of the play, except for the tempest itself, takes place on the island. It conforms to the unity of action because all of the events are directly relevant to the central plotline. Prospero's desire to make his enemies penitent, regain what is rightfully his and set the scene for a peaceful future is inextricably linked to the sub-plots involving Alonso's group and Stephano's group. He is also very close to being an **omniscient** character; because he is aware of what everyone on the island is doing, he is able to adjust his plans accordingly. Most importantly, *The Tempest* also conforms to the unity of time. Roughly speaking, the action of the play takes place in 'real time' and unfolds within a single afternoon. We are told that the play begins 'At least two glasses' past noon (I.2.240) and as it reaches its close in Act V scene 1, Ariel declares the time to be 'On the sixth hour' (4). Without any significant cutting, the play might be expected to run for something close to this four-hour period, probably including an interval.

Dramatic advantages

Because real time and dramatic time correspond fairly closely to one another, we share Prospero's sense of urgency to accomplish his plans before the allotted deadline. He breaks off the spirit masque which he conjures up for Miranda and Ferdinand in Act IV scene 1, as he suddenly realises that 'The minute' of Caliban, Stephano and Trinculo's plan has arrived (141). Only at the start of Act V, when all his plans are in hand, does he acknowledge that 'time/Goes upright with his carriage' (2–3), no longer burdened by the weight of uncompleted tasks. He also acknowledges the dangers of executing his plans so quickly. He sets Ferdinand the task of working as his slave, arguing that it is an effective love test (I.2.451–53):

> ...this swift business
> I must uneasy make, lest too light winning
> Make the prize light.

Furthermore, it could be argued that conforming to the unity of time lends a sense of realism to a fantastical plot; although we may be in a strange land which abounds with outlandish characters and magical powers, the world of the play does at least observe the laws of time. This allows the audience to suspend disbelief for the duration of the play.

The past

Despite the fact that the play is set over a short period of time, we are told a great deal about the characters' lives prior to the events we witness. Here is a list of the actions we are told about during the play which take place before it starts:

- **Prospero** is usurped as Duke of Milan in a plot laid by Antonio and Alonso.
- **Miranda** is banished along with her father, landing on the island at the age of three. She has only the vaguest recollections of seeing any humans other than Prospero.
- **Caliban** is born to the witch Sycorax, and she dies 12 years later. Another 12 years on, Prospero lands on the island and adopts him. Caliban shows Prospero all the beauty and fertility of the island and is rewarded by being taught how to speak by Miranda. However, he then attempts to rape her and is made Prospero's slave as punishment.
- **Ariel** is confined to a pine tree by one of Sycorax's spells. Prospero rescues Ariel and makes the sprite his servant.
- **Alonso** conspires with Antonio to usurp Prospero as the Duke of Milan. He also agrees to the marriage of his daughter Claribel to the King of Tunis, thus weakening his line of descent to the throne of Naples.
- **Antonio** usurps Prospero, taking his place as Duke of Milan.
- **Gonzalo** took pity on Prospero and Miranda when they were expelled from from Milan. He provided food, water, clothes and Prospero's magic books, which enabled him to survive the journey at sea and the subsequent 12-year period on the island.

The time scheme

A running time of four hours is a long time, particularly for a modern audience, which might be frustrated by the slow unfolding of the action. There is certainly a sense that some of the scenes involving Trinculo and Stephano are slightly super-fluous, though they can offer welcome comic interludes in the play.

The time scheme also causes problems for the maintenance of **verisimilitude**. Miranda and Ferdinand only meet halfway through the play and yet they are engaged to be married in a very short space of time. Despite Prospero setting a love

test for Ferdinand, this could suggest that their relationship is built on unsound foundations, especially considering the fact that Miranda has never seen any other man apart from her father and Caliban. It is also unrealistic to believe that the repentance of Alonso (and in particular of Antonio and Sebastian) will last, given that it has occurred so quickly. Gonzalo claims in Act V scene 1 that 'all of us' have found 'ourselves' (212), having learned the importance of virtue through their experiences on the island. Though this may be true of some characters, it is hardly a plausible claim to make of all of them, particularly in the light of the uneasy silences of Antonio and Sebastian in the final scene.

The ending of *The Tempest* is as open as that of any of Shakespeare's plays, and this is — at least in part — a result of his conformity to the unity of time.

Fantasy or realism?

The Tempest conforms fairly closely to Aristotle's three **unities**, which are usually employed to judge whether or not a play is realistic. However, the basic subject matter of *The Tempest* is so fantastical that the play itself cannot really be considered realistic in its fullest sense. Instead, the unities offer a surface realism which allows us to immerse ourselves in a world very different from our own. Although Prospero's magic allows him to bend all sorts of scientific laws, he is still subject to the basic demands of time and place. He cannot travel through time and his power has not allowed him to leave the island before the action of the play starts. As mentioned earlier, Shakespeare's conformity to the unities allows us to suspend disbelief as we watch the play, although it does not mean that we are led to believe that the sorts of magical acts that take place in the play could happen in real life. Nonetheless, we should consider that a Jacobean audience would have been much more superstitious about witchcraft and the supernatural than we are today. They might therefore have given more credence to Prospero's 'magical' powers than a modern audience.

Magic, witchcraft and the supernatural

In the early seventeenth century people were much more superstitious than they are today, and there was widespread belief in the occult and the paranormal. It was believed that evil spirits were omnipresent, waiting for humans to give in to temptation and thus incur damnation. In *Hamlet* the young prince expresses concern that the ghost of his father, who appears to him and begs him to kill his uncle, may in fact be a devil trying to lure him into hell. It was also believed that witches made a pact with the devil, thereby gaining satanic powers. In Christopher Marlowe's *Dr Faustus* (1588) the protagonist performs exactly this rite, signing his soul away to Mephistopheles in exchange for supernatural powers.

Daemonologie

James I, who ascended the throne in 1603, was a staunch believer in the dangerous satanic power of black magic. He wrote a book, entitled *Daemonologie*, which contained a strict anti-magic ideology. In this atmosphere of fear and suspicion, many people were tried for and convicted of witchcraft. The witchcraft statute of 1563 decreed that witches could not be hanged for a first offence unless it brought about the death of their victim. However, this legislation was changed in 1604, shortly after James became king. Even at his coronation, when he proclaimed a general amnesty, James was careful to exclude criminals in witchcraft from this show of magnanimity. The number of convictions for witchcraft over the next decade rose extremely rapidly.

Persecution

The persecution of people considered to be witches was a form of scapegoating which grew out of social and economic discontent. It was not uncommon for events such as a bad crop or livestock dying to be blamed on the curses of a witch. In an age when disease was not well understood and education was scant among the general population, medical disasters were often attributed to the ill will of an unpopular local individual rather than to any more scientific cause.

Witch trials continued to take place throughout the seventeenth century, and the proceedings of these trials are available to examine in legal accounts, which are preserved to this day. Evidence was often very flimsy, and it sometimes took little more than hearsay or particularly vehement prosecution by a few individuals to convict defendants as witches. Even King James's hard-line attitude to witches had its limits, however. He denounced as a fraud a boy whose testimony led to the conviction of nine women — but not before their punishment of hanging had been carried out.

It is worth noting that accusations of witchery were usually targeted at women, and particularly those who suffered from some sort of physical abnormality. In an age rife with misogyny, it was believed that outer appearance often reflected inner nature, and women who did not conform to social conventions were at particular risk of being denounced as witches. There was also a great deal of mystery surrounding the physical functions of women (menstrual periods are still sometimes known **colloquially** as 'the curse'), and women were considered less rational than men and subject to behaviour which could not be explained logically.

The sceptic Reginald Scot tried to dispel several popular conceptions about witches and witchcraft in his book *Discoverie of Witchcraft* (1584), but his arguments

were attacked by King James. The king's insistence on the power of witches — which, he claimed, were obtained though a pact with Satan — further legitimised belief in the power of supernatural forces.

The Tempest and magic

Against this background of suspicion about magic and the supernatural, the character of Prospero is particularly susceptible to negative interpretation. Despite exhibiting great power, he is careful not to show **hubris**, thanking 'Providence divine' for delivering his enemies to him and swiftly giving up his magical powers at the end of the play. Shakespeare also contrasts Prospero's relatively benign brand of magic with the evil 'black' magic of Sycorax, who represents the damage magic can cause in the wrong hands. The fact that Prospero undermines her magic, freeing Ariel from the pine tree in which she imprisoned him and exercising power over her son Caliban, indicates that he is a balancing figure who is only using his powers to restore the 'natural' or rightful order of things.

Magic is generally defined as that which cannot be explained in scientific or 'natural' terms. Prospero is very careful to divert attention away from his own extraordinary powers and onto Caliban, a character who does not conform to 'natural' laws of what a man should be. His lust for Miranda culminates in his trans-gression of trying to rape her, and Prospero labels him as a 'devil', 'misshapen' and 'disproportioned'. His appearance to the other characters certainly exhibits the hallmarks of a 'devil'. In this sense Caliban is more supernatural than Prospero, who manifests his naturalness in his love of his daughter and his desire to restore the 'natural' order to society by crushing his enemies and regaining his rightful throne. Prospero employs a vocabulary of abnormality when referring to Caliban, while emphasising the normality of his own desires and goals, thus directing the audience's attention away from his supernatural powers.

The Epilogue, though often cut from performances of the play, also serves the important purpose of showing Prospero humble and powerless without his magic; he deserves our pity because he has given up the powers which brought him the status of a demi-god, powers which would allow him to fulfil any ambition he were to choose. In this sense he is turning away from the temptations which corrupted the likes of Alonso, Antonio, Sebastian, Stephano and Trinculo — perhaps the greatest of all the feats he accomplishes during the action of the play.

Art and illusion

Illusion has to do with the gap between how things appear and how they really are. Those episodes where characters disagree about what is real and what is not are therefore crucial to this theme. Gonzalo claims in Act II scene 1 that his clothes are no longer stained with sea salt, as if they have been magically laundered. He is roundly mocked by Antonio and Sebastian, who do not believe that such a supernatural occurrence is possible. Their disagreement extends to their views of the island, which Gonzalo and Adrian find green and fragrant and Sebastian and Antonio see as barren. These wildly different views underline the fact that all experience is subjective, and that our concept of reality is closely tied to our own perspective. When Miranda first sets eyes on Ferdinand, for example, she cries: 'I might call him/A thing divine, for nothing natural/I ever saw so noble' (I.2.418–20). Prospero retorts that she is in no position to judge, having seen so few men, and that 'To th'most of men this is a Caliban,/And they to him are angels' (I.2.481–82). Prospero is, of course, lying, but he nonetheless makes the valid point that beauty, like so many other human qualities — and even our concept of reality — is often judged by comparison.

The sense of illusion is overpowering in Act V scene 1 when Alonso sees Prospero, whom for 12 years he has thought dead. He declares: 'Whe'er thou beest he or no,/Or some enchanted trifle to abuse me,/As late I have been, I not know' (111–13). However, he describes how 'Th'affliction of my mind amends' (115), suggesting that he is returning to reality, no matter how strange that reality may seem. A few lines later Gonzalo still expresses scepticism, stating: 'Whether this be/Or not be, I'll not swear' (122–23), and this confusion is compounded by the revelation of Miranda and Ferdinand playing chess in Prospero's cell. The tone of Sebastian's voice as he proclaims this another 'most high miracle' (177) is probably sarcastic; compared with all the recent miracles, this occurrence seems almost normal.

The island is a magical place, where the rules of the outside world can be broken at will by Prospero and his followers. We must constantly question the reality of events on the stage — and even of our own existence, as Prospero implies when he states that 'We are such stuff/As dreams are made on' (IV.1.156–57).

Themes

Many of the themes of *The Tempest* are built into the structure of the play so that, for instance, the interpolation of the masque scene illustrates that theatre is itself an illusion. When the themes of the play are considered together, Shakespeare seems to be preoccupied with issues of order. He explores the social hierarchies of class, gender and race, while also considering magic and music as agents of restoring peace and harmony. The 'natural' order of politics, love and family is a further overarching concern in *The Tempest*, relating to issues of service and usurpation as well as the power of love (and lust) to create and to destroy established loyalties.

Illusion

Illusion is closely tied to the theme of magic, but is not synonymous with it. Ariel and Prospero appear invisible to, or concealed from, the other characters on several

occasions. This creates a sense of **dramatic irony**: we feel immediately that there is a gap between what we as the audience see and what the different characters are aware of. At the end of the play Gonzalo expresses his bafflement by asserting: 'Whether this be/Or be not, I'll not swear' (V.1.122–23). For Gonzalo, like his companions, so many incredible events have occurred that it is difficult to know whether any, all or none of them are real.

The theme of illusion causes us to question our own role as the audience of an artificial theatrical construct. After the masque scene in Act IV scene 1 Prospero compares life to the 'pageant' we have just witnessed, suggesting that both are transient: 'We are such stuff/As dreams are made on; and our little life/Is rounded with a sleep' (156–58). The play-within-a-play — as well as the setting of the play in the **microcosm** of a remote island — leaves us to consider the very nature of theatre, and to ask whether our own existence is any more real than the action we see on the stage before us.

Usurpation

Usurpation is the central theme of two of the sub-plots, the main plot and events which happened before the play begins. It is the overarching theme of the play, suggesting that humans are inherently greedy, ambitious and power hungry. The plots of Antonio, Alonso, Sebastian, Caliban, Stephano and Trinculo are motivated by a range of easily identifiable human feelings, but there are less clear-cut cases of usurpation. Prospero usurps Caliban's place on the island, and Ferdinand usurps Prospero's role as the predominant male figure in Miranda's life. Usurpation is the assumption of a role which is not rightfully, or 'naturally' your own. The theme therefore feeds into the idea that the word is in chaos, and must be returned to a state of order to prevent further 'unnatural' disasters from occurring.

Colonialism

Colonialism is explored in the play through the power relations between characters and the varying degrees to which they influence one another. It is related to issues of usurpation and service, and entails the appropriation of land and culture — all issues which were, and still are, of great political importance. Perhaps the key aspect of this theme to analyse is whether the European characters are a 'civilising' influence on the natives of the island or a corrupting one. Is the island a Garden of Eden which is shattered by the arrival of a domineering Western force? Do we agree with Prospero that he is justified in ruling the island despite landing on it after Ariel and Caliban? Does Ariel owe Prospero his service or is he compelled to serve by a powerful imperialist force? However you view these issues, colonialism is at the heart of the play's power structures, its morality, and the cultural and historical contexts in which it is performed.

Music

The musical aspects of the play enliven the entertainment, but they also have serious thematic implications. Music is conveyed through the element of air, and is primarily Ariel's medium: he sings, plays tunes on his pipe and dances. As Prospero's servant he can be seen as the medium of his conductor's wishes, helping Prospero to build harmony from the discordant feelings of love and hate in circulation on the island. Music can therefore be seen as a metaphor for the play, and a vehicle for magic powers; Ariel sends characters to sleep with music, and, like the pied piper, leads them from one end of the island to the other with his charming airs. Music also restores order and peace in place of the chaotic, drunken singing of Caliban and his crew.

Reconciliation

The Tempest is one of Shakespeare's **romances**, and one of the conventions of the genre is that potentially tragic events end in resolution rather than destruction. Instead of taking revenge on those who have wronged him, Prospero chooses to show leniency, forgiving his enemies and building a more stable future for everyone. The genre of revenge tragedies, which were popular at the time, invariably ended up with a large proportion of the cast dead, as we see in Shakespeare's *Hamlet*, because each act of vengeance spawned another.

Family

The theme of family is closely related to ideas of 'nature' and behaving 'naturally'. Antonio's original usurpation of Prospero caused Miranda to consider that 'Good wombs have borne bad sons' (I.2.120); the 'natural' family instincts of loyalty and protectiveness are clearly missing from the make-up of her uncle's character. Sebastian proves an interesting parallel in this respect, claiming that he will use Antonio's successful coup as his 'precedent' and setting out to murder his own brother, Alonso, in Act II scene 1 (296).

Caliban, the 'demi-devil', is defined by his birth to the witch Sycorax. It was believed that witches indulged in sexual union with Satan, and Caliban — as Sycorax's offspring — is therefore defined by the circumstances of his conception. This is a theme which runs through Shakespearean drama; in *King Lear* Gloucester's bastard son Edmund betrays his father, while his legitimate son Edgar is loyal and faithful in spite of the false allegations which are made against him.

Family ties also dictate the political landscape of *The Tempest*. Ferdinand's marriage to Miranda is advantageous because it brings together Milan and Naples, thus ensuring that an atmosphere of peace and prosperity can develop in the future. In Act II scene 1 Antonio points out to Sebastian that Claribel, having married the King of Tunis, 'dwells/Ten leagues beyond man's life' (250–51). This is an exaggerated way of saying that she is out of reach of Naples in the event that Alonso should die; with Ferdinand presumed dead, Sebastian is therefore next in line to the throne.

Otherness

Otherness is a theme which runs through several of Shakespeare's plays — most notably those which feature black characters, like *Othello* and *Titus Andronicus*. Both Othello and Aaron are Moors in Western white society, and are discriminated against because of the colour of their skin. Caliban, however, is abused and enslaved despite having been born on the island. In this sense the concept of being an outsider is a flexible one; is it Prospero and the other Europeans who are aliens, or the humanoid Caliban, whose outward appearance marks him out as different even though he is in his homeland? This theme is closely related to colonialism, the ownership of culture and language, and the nature of man.

Betrayal

Betrayal takes place where a band of trust or love is ignored, usually in favour of self-advancement. The theme of betrayal runs through every aspect of the play, though sometimes in less malevolent forms than might be expected. Prospero is betrayed by his brother Antonio, who in turn betrays his partner in crime, Alonso. He does so by teaming up with Alonso's brother, Sebastian — yet another character willing to undo his own family. Caliban betrays the trust of Prospero in his attempt to rape Miranda, while it could be argued that Prospero committed the ultimate betrayal on the island by dispossessing Caliban of his rightful kingdom. Miranda seems to betray her father by breaking his rules and courting Ferdinand behind his back, although in reality, Prospero approves and engineers the match from the start.

Revenge

Revenge is a hateful impulse, which is the inverse of reconciliation and forgiveness. Prospero avenges himself (though with a great degree of restraint) on Antonio and Alonso; Caliban pursues murderous redress against Prospero until he is thwarted in his aims; both Sebastian and Antonio seem at the end of the play to be biding their time before targeting Prospero once more. In the midst of this proliferation of hatred, Shakespeare demonstrates that the only way to break the cycle of vengeance is to show forgiveness. In the end Prospero chooses to show mercy to his enemies, offering them a place in a new and peaceful social order.

Love and sex

Love comes in many different forms in the play, from Miranda and Ferdinand's romantic love to the filial love they both feel towards their fathers. Caliban is cast out of Prospero's cell for his inability to control his sexual desire for Miranda. In this sense he is on the same level as Stephano, who is motivated to kill Prospero by Caliban's tales of Miranda's beauty before he has even seen her. The paternal love which Alonso and Prospero exhibit for their children underlines the potential sorrow of losing one's child in marriage (as Alonso loses Claribel); Prospero is fortunate to feel that he has gained a son in Ferdinand rather than having lost his daughter. In the end the purest or most 'natural' forms of love triumph and endure; families are reunited, an engagement takes place and the base characters are punished for their destructive impulses.

Service

Service is a theme which can be interpreted to include both slavery and voluntary servitude. It is a concept which is integral to Christianity and feudalism (a legal and social system from Medieval times, whereby lords granted land to people who served them), as well as to the social and family structures of the period. Every social group has a hierarchy, but the anarchy of the enchanted island causes many characters in the play to think they can transfer themselves to a higher social level. Prospero installs himself as ruler of the island through his superior powers and then creates resentment by forcing Caliban into his service and extracting a promise of duty from Ariel. This resentment boils over into mutinous thoughts, which are shared by the lower-class characters of Stephano the butler and Trinculo the jester. The sub-plots portray man as a creature who desires liberty but also hankers after the power to enslave others. Service requires humility and acceptance of hierarchy, and those who have too much pride cannot bear to be servants. The master–servant relationship was considered crucial to an understanding of humanity and its roles and was the expression of the civilising virtues of nobility, trust, loyalty, honour, love and harmony.

The elements

In Shakespeare's time, audiences would have been aware of the hierarchy of the four different elements (earth, air, fire and water) and the connotations each of them held. Caliban is associated with the lowest of the elements, earth, while Alonso's party are forced to abandon the sea (water) and return to solid ground themselves. It is only at the end of the play that they are allowed to return to the sea, while Caliban probably remains on the island. Likewise, Prospero's return to humanity is signalled by his decision to give up his magic, which consists of the fiery sprites in the air, and travel back to Italy by boat. Between them, Prospero and Ariel control all four elements, as we see in the conjuring of the tempest (consisting of lightning, wind and rain) and Prospero's dominion over the earth-bound Caliban. As such, they hold sway over all the other characters in the play.

Imagery

Shakespeare's imagery repays close study, as each play has its own peculiar group of recurring images in addition to the typical and traditional images of the Elizabethan period, such as those pertaining to heaven and hell, fire and water, light and dark,

bonds and divisions. The language of the romances is dominated by images of birth and rebirth, fertility and natural abundance.

In Shakespeare's plays, images are often literalised **metaphors**. For example, Prospero refers to Caliban as 'this thing of darkness' (V.1.275), describing both his skin colour and his supposedly evil nature. In addition to reinforcing themes, imagery gives atmosphere and progression to a text, helps to delineate character and provides integrity, pattern and meaning. The images used in *The Tempest* vary between characters, as each sees something different; for some, the fertility of the island is as palpable as its barrenness is to others, for example. The result is a clash of linguistic registers, as the imagery of hell permeates that of the gods, human intellect is juxtaposed with animalistic impulses, and so on. The wildly different pictures different characters paint of themselves and the island suggest that it is a world of subjectivity, where everything can be interpreted in a huge number of ways, and no stable, unchanging view of it is offered.

Gods/the heavens

Most characters in the play make references to the gods and fate, which is usually an indication that they feel events are out of their control. The gods offer stability and meaning, because events can always be interpreted as the work of a divine being. However, some characters are more inclined to make these references than others, and for different reasons.

Miranda thanks the 'heavens' for her safe arrival on the island (I.2.175). Prospero also shows his gratitude to 'Providence divine' (I.2.159) for looking after him at sea and to 'bountiful Fortune' (I.2.178) for bringing his enemies to him. These references show Prospero as graciously aware of the limits of his own powers, and unwilling to aspire to godlike status himself. Caliban, who begs Stephano to release him from Prospero's service, seems to be searching for another idol to serve. He begins by taking a drink from Stephano's bottle and exclaiming, 'the liquor is not earthly' (II.2.123), then asks: 'Hast thou not dropped from heaven?' (II.2.134). Stephano offers him the bottle as if it were a Bible, commanding him to 'Kiss the book' (139), and by the end of the scene Caliban is begging to be ruled over: 'I prithee, be my god' (146). Alonso too looks for evidence of divine influence to explain events; when he is reunited with Ferdinand, he looks at Miranda and asks: 'Is she the goddess that hath severed us,/And brought us thus together?' (V.1.187–88). The imagery of gods and heavenliness thus infuses all aspects of *The Tempest*, alluding to Shakespeare's own role as god in the world of the play, and to the divine order of life itself.

Words

The numerous references to words, speech, cursing, oaths and wordplay remind us that the play revolves around words and the way they are used. Prospero's long speech to Miranda in Act I indicates that she is to be seen and not heard, like all obedient women of the time. Caliban's command of language defines him as a poetic 'noble savage', superior to the prose-speaking likes of Stephano and Trinculo. The 'dumb discourse' (III.3.40) of Prospero's sprites who 'want the use of tongue' (III.3.39) contributes to the mystery surrounding events on the island.

Eyes

At the end of the play Alonso and Gonzalo can hardly believe their eyes. Having witnessed an illusory banquet appear and disappear, Ferdinand returning unscathed to join them, and Prospero's apparent resurrection, they can only conclude that their senses are deceiving them. Ariel and Prospero appear to the audience but unseen to the other characters on stage throughout the play, throwing into doubt the meaning of even the simplest of conversations. By the end of the play we — like Gonzalo — are forced to shrug our shoulders and assert: 'Whether this be/Or be not, I'll not swear' (V.1.122–23).

Time

In Act V scene 1 Prospero describes how 'time/Goes upright with his carriage' (2–3) as his plan comes to fruition. By personifying time as a character who acts independently of Prospero, Shakespeare highlights that this is one of the few things on the island which the magus cannot control. In fact, the whole play is an exercise in shedding light on events which happened in 'the dark and backward abysm of time' (I.2.50) in order that openness, peace and prosperity can be opened up in the future.

Food/eating

In Shakespeare's day gluttony was regarded by the Church as one of the **seven deadly sins**. Caliban declares 'I must eat my dinner' in Act I scene 2, showing the compulsive appetites of a primitive creature. Eating was associated with bestial appetites and was considered a low activity from which higher beings with spiritual aspirations were supposed to refrain as much as possible (or at least they were not to talk about it). Thus the imagery of Alonso rejecting Gonzalo's rambling speeches ('You cram these words into mine ears, against/The stomach of my sense' (II.1.108–09)), and of the sea spitting the Italians up onto the island, associates these characters with excessive behaviour, albeit in different ways. The illusory banquet with which Ariel tantalises Alonso's group plays on religious associations with food once again; some critics argue that the food represents communion, which the group (containing several unrepentant sinners) is not yet ready to receive.

Hell

From the moment Ferdinand abandons ship crying, 'Hell is empty,/And all the devils are here!' (I.2.214–15), the characters in the play attribute various unpleasant

or supernatural occurrences to Satan. As the offspring of the witch Sycorax, Caliban is termed 'A devil, a born devil' (IV.1.188) and is associated with blackness (possibly because of his skin colour); Prospero dubs him 'this thing of darkness' (V.1.275). While all the characters are ready to see evil spirits in their surroundings, Prospero wisely asserts in Act III scene 3 that 'some of you there present/Are worse than devils' (36–37); it is certainly ambiguous where the real evil in the play resides.

Disease

This is the language of cursing on the island, with Caliban calling on the 'red plague' (I.2.364) and 'infections' to rain on Prospero in order to 'make him/By inch-meal a disease!' (II.2.1–3). Prospero too summons 'cramps' and 'Side-stitches' against his enemies (I.2.325–26), while Stephano thinks that the moaning Caliban is an islander suffering from the ague. In stark contrast, Prospero also describes how Miranda is 'infected' by love for Ferdinand; this was a common metaphor at the time, encapsulating the uncontrollable nature of love and the physical symptoms accompanying it, which sometimes bore a resemblance to those of illness.

Music

In Act I scene 2 Prospero describes how Antonio 'set all hearts i'th'state/To what tune pleased his ear' (84–85) in order to depose him as Duke of Milan. This metaphor is particularly apt because musical imagery in the play tells us a great deal about who is in control of the action at different points. Ariel leads Caliban's drunken group through thorns and swamps with his magical tunes, and brings Ferdinand and Alonso's group to Prospero's cell. Music is an integral part of the island itself, embodied in the character of Ariel, the other sprites, and even in Caliban's reeling and drunken song. As he explains in Act III scene 2: 'the isle is full of noises,/Sounds, and sweet airs, that give delight and hurt not' (136–37). The sense of wonder and spectacle is transmitted to the audience through the fabulous imagery of 'twangling instruments' (III.2.138) and the complementary sound of music on stage.

Fertility

Nature contains life and death, fertility and decay, and the way each character speaks of what the island has to offer tells us more about them than their surroundings. For those who are in tune with it, the island abounds with produce and life. Caliban knows the fresh water sources and where to find berries, apples, fish and eggs, among other things. In contrast, Antonio and Sebastian see only a barren and unpleasant land that yields nothing but 'rotten' air (II.1.50). The masque scene in Act IV celebrates marital union and childbirth, as the sprites evoke Hymen, the goddess of marriage. Ceres and Iris also harness the imagery of seasonal change (which was commonly linked to ideas of birth and rebirth in Shakespeare) in order to bless Ferdinand and Miranda's marriage with fertility.

Bondage

The distinction between service and slavery in the play is a fine one, and one that seems to be governed by the attitude each character brings to it. Ferdinand sees his 'labours' (III.1.7) at the behest of Prospero as pleasurable service of Miranda. Ariel is at first unwilling to follow Prospero, using the language of compulsion to describe their relationship. However, he realises this is against his best interests, throwing himself into his duties and reaping Prospero's praise where Caliban receives only abuse. To some degree, then, slavery and service are portrayed as two sides of the same coin — though one is infinitely more attractive than the other.

Animals

The animal/man division on which Shakespeare often draws in order to comment on the bestial aspects of mankind is made more complex in *The Tempest* by the presence of Caliban. Miranda explains how he used to 'gabble like/A thing most brutish' (I.2.356–57), showing that, in terms of the chain of being, Caliban is not easily defined. This raises the fundamental question of what makes a man. Caliban bemoans the 'urchin-shows', 'apes', 'hedgehogs' and 'adders' (II.2.5–13) which Prospero sends to punish his disobedience. These menacing, poisonous or prickly creatures are in marked contrast to the produce of bountiful nature Caliban mentions later, the 'jay's nest', 'marmoset', 'clust'ring filberts' and 'Young scamels' (II.2.166–69). This contrast shows that, like men, animals can be both kind and malevolent, and perhaps suggests that a noble savage like Caliban may even be superior to base and brutish men like Stephano and Trinculo.

The sea

The sea is an elemental force which underlines the powerlessness of man to determine his own destiny. It is a dangerous and chaotic image of uncertainty which sets the events of the play in motion by plucking the characters from their ship with total ease, and constitutes a barrier between the island and the rest of the world. The storm-tossed sea, though controlled by Prospero, symbolises nature's dissatisfaction with the order of the universe, where virtue has been punished and evil has triumphed up until the start of the play. As it is in a constant state of tidal change, the sea also represents flux and transformation. The phrase 'sea change' means a significant alteration in the state of someone/something, much like the moral change that occurs in Alonso (and arguably some of the other characters) by the end of the play.

Music and masque

The Tempest is the most musical of Shakespeare's plays, and it can be an audiovisual extravaganza if sufficient emphasis is placed on this element. Ideally, the roles of Ariel and the island's sprites should be played by skilled musicians and dancers in order to realise the thematic and theatrical potential of the music. The songs in the play perform a range of functions, from pure entertainment to the exploration of character and the progression of the plot.

Equally importantly, *The Tempest* has much in common with the masque form. The 'pageant' of the kind that Prospero stages in Act IV scene 1 (155) is a crucial analogue to the play's themes and issues. Masques tended to be performed at court to celebrate events like births and marriages, and were lavish productions, designed to show off the wealth and opulence of the monarch. They often featured ornate costumes, fantastical settings, elaborate verse and many of the themes of romance, such as regeneration and transformation. Our understanding of the play is therefore greatly enriched by a detailed knowledge of the theatrical context in which the play was performed.

The dramatic effect of music

The music of the play serves several purposes. On a practical level, the songs provide entertaining interludes in the story. Such set pieces, if performed by a skilled musician and accompanied by good chorography, offer a whole new dimension to the play. Theatre in the sixteenth and seventeenth centuries was often broken up with gambling, bear-baiting and other entertainments, so the music would have contributed to a general atmosphere of merry-making.

The music also gives the island an aura of magic, mystery and 'otherness'. Ferdinand's first response to Ariel's song in Act I scene 2 encapsulates this; he says in wonder: 'Where should this music be? I'th'air, or th'earth?' (388). The island takes on an ethereal quality, like a world suspended somewhere between the heavens and reality.

Singing sprites

Ariel is the central musician in the play, and is responsible for singing the majority of the songs. He and his sprites are very much an organic part of the environment of the play, a setting in which music and magic go hand in hand. By singing, Ariel is fulfilling his natural role as a musical spirit, creating an atmosphere of peace and harmony. On the other hand, his songs are effectively dictated to him by the demands Prospero makes. They tend to have strongly accentuated rhythms and obvious rhyme schemes, giving the impression of order and ritual. The songs can therefore be interpreted either as a means for Ariel to express himself, or as another agent of Prospero's control over him.

This dichotomy is also evident in Caliban's songs, for they represent his joy at the possibility of being free but also his continuing enslavement (to Stephano, if his plot against Prospero succeeds). Even though Caliban was born on the island, he was conceived in Africa, and in this sense is not a 'natural' musician like Ariel and the sprites. His drunken revels can be seen as a grotesque parody of the sprites' 'sweet airs' (III.2.137) and are discordant with the harmonies which represent Prospero's power.

Hearing as harmony

Because music was considered a symbol of divine and universal harmony in Jacobean times, those who were unable to hear it can be interpreted as existing outside this order. In Act II scene 1 Gonzalo and the other courtiers hear Ariel's music and succumb to sleep. Alonso then becomes drowsy, while Antonio and Sebastian stay awake and plot his murder. Shakespeare presents us with a sliding scale of goodness here, where sinful men are less able to hear sources of natural harmony than virtuous ones, as if they are out of tune with nature itself. As if to emphasise this point, Ariel re-enters, waking Gonzalo with another song just in time to thwart the treacherous plan. At the start of Act V scene 1 Prospero renounces his magic in order to establish a stable and harmonious political order. It is symbolic that his pursuit of peace is accompanied by his call for 'Some heavenly music' (52).

Music as power

In Act I scene 2 Prospero laments how Antonio 'set all hearts i'th'state/To what tune pleased his ear' (84–85), acting as a conductor of affairs and thereby succeeding in winning his brother's throne. On the island these roles are reversed, as Prospero directs a cast of musical sprites to do his bidding. Ariel is chief among these, and his songs are a symbol both of his magical power and of his servitude; though he enjoys leading the other characters around the island with his tunes, his music is a vehicle for Prospero's plans. Caliban's few songs reveal a similar trend. At the end of Act II scene 2 he sings in joyful expectation of Prospero's death, but he is only really celebrating the fact that he has found a new master in Stephano. Caliban celebrates the island's 'sweet airs' (III.2.137) and 'twangling instruments' (III.2.138) but seems unaware that the songs which send him to sleep are another means by which Prospero controls him. Ultimately, Ferdinand is quite right when he assumes that the music he hears 'waits upon/Some god o'th'island' (I.2.389–90). The incantatory nature of the songs' rhythms and rhyme schemes makes them sound like magic spells, which, in effect, they are.

The masque

The masque scene at first seems so different from the style of the rest of the play as to bear little relevance to it. However, its symbolic value is clear. The affected and

formal **rhyming couplets** are typical of masques of the time, exaggerating the artificial nature of the performance and suggesting that its value lies beneath the surface. The masque constitutes an effective **allegory** which allows Prospero to raise issues which he may be embarrassed to mention to Ferdinand and Miranda, or unwilling to repeat again.

Ceres and Juno are pleased by the absence of Venus and Cupid (agents of sexual desire), as this communicates the importance of chastity and purity. This echoes Prospero's repeated injunctions that Ferdinand refrain from making sexual advances to Miranda before they are married. However, as a goddess of fertility, Ceres also evokes images of agricultural plenty which relate to the fruitfulness of the marriage bed. It is crucial to Prospero's plans that Miranda has a strong line of legitimate descendants. The threatening figure of 'dusky Dis' (who raped Proserpina in Roman mythology) can be seen to represent the dark-skinned Caliban, whose earlier attempt to rape Miranda threatened her purity.

The images of agricultural plenty bring to mind the theme of good husbandry, or looking after one's land. Given that Ferdinand and Miranda will one day rule over both Milan and Naples, this is a telling allusion. Prospero uses the masque as a way of encoding his best wishes for Ferdinand and Miranda's happiness together, as well as a method of offering them sensible advice about their future responsibilities. The contrast between barren and fertile land is pertinent because it simultaneously communicates the importance of pre-marital chastity and of bearing heirs once married.

Revenge and repentance

At the time that Shakespeare was writing *The Tempest*, revenge tragedy was a popular genre. Two of the most famous examples of these sorts of plays were Shakespeare's own *Hamlet* (1602) and Thomas Kyd's *The Spanish Tragedy* (1592). Revenge was an Old Testament value, inspired by the paradigm of 'an eye for an eye, a tooth for a tooth'. Revenge tragedies inevitably ended with a stage full of corpses and the powerful message that a cycle of revenge will only end up damning all those who become a part of it. *The Tempest* conveys a much more conciliatory message, based on the New Testament values of turning the other cheek and showing mercy and forgiveness.

One of the key issues of the play, however, is whether Prospero's magnanimous approach to meting out punishment to his enemies is either productive or fair. Some critics believe that Antonio and Sebastian are unrepentant for their actions, and that Caliban's greatest regret is not that he attempted to murder his master but that he failed in the attempt. Furthermore, Prospero's entitlement to dispense justice must be called into question. Is he totally guiltless, or must he too take a share of the blame for the scenes of bloodlust and deception we have witnessed?

Alonso the penitent

Some critics argue that Alonso was already repenting before he even arrived on the island. It is certainly true that as early as Act I scene 1 Gonzalo declares that 'The King and Prince [are] at prayers' (52), in expectation that they will die in the shipwreck. This suggests that Alonso has an active conscience, unlike Antonio and Sebastian. In fact, his actions throughout the play suggest that he regrets many decisions he has made. In Act II scene 1 he wishes he had never married his daughter to the King of Tunis. The wedding trip has now turned into a disaster, with Ferdinand seemingly dead too. Alonso is in a melancholic state, unwilling to listen to others' chatter and apparently deep in thought. When Ariel appears as a harpy with the banquet in Act III scene 3, and chastises the 'three men of sin' for usurping Prospero, Alonso gives up on the possibility that Ferdinand might have survived the shipwreck and wishes to lie dead with his son, as if to acknowledge his guilt. Ariel's words merely substantiate Alonso's belief that Ferdinand's death is a just punishment for the sins he committed before the action of the play.

Poetic justice

Poetic justice can be described as 'the due allocation of reward and punishment for virtue and vice respectively'. The question of whether *The Tempest* fulfils this definition largely depends on whether students believe that 'good' and 'bad' characters can be identified unambiguously. Virtue, in the form of Miranda and Ferdinand, is portrayed as something which attracts its own reward, as the two characters pair off with one another. Where vice is concerned, meanwhile, Prospero is the figure who metes out punishment or forgiveness throughout the play, and yet he is never subject to judgement himself, except by the audience in the Epilogue. Our interpretation of whether Caliban is fairly punished for his attempted murder of Prospero is influenced by whether we think he had just motives for undertaking it in the first place.

It could be argued that *The Tempest* does not conform to the definition of poetic justice because the most evil characters are not treated much differently from the most virtuous. Prospero's emphasis on forgiveness at the close of the play suggests that many of the sins committed, by Antonio and Sebastian in particular, have been forgotten before their perpetrators have been forced to repent for their actions. A series of attempted murders has taken place, and yet punishment has amounted to little more than a few frightening illusions in the course of a single afternoon. Antonio loses his dukedom, which seems fair, but is not punished further for his murderous plots. Sebastian had little to lose in the first place, and Alonso is still unaware that his own brother intended to kill him (though Prospero warns Sebastian that he may yet reveal this fact at a later date). The clowns Stephano and Trinculo are punished by being forced to tidy Prospero's cell, but this somewhat comic punishment conceals the fact that they intended to murder

Prospero in cold blood; in this sense their punishment is woefully inadequate as a deterrent against future plots.

Prospero the penitent?

An analysis of Prospero's crimes reveals that he is willing to accept some of his faults but is in total denial about others. He concedes that he was not a diligent enough ruler when Duke of Milan, and that he should have discharged his duties with more care. However, he never apologises to Caliban for the way he has treated him, apparently because he believes that his punishments were all justified. He is in total control over proceedings on the island, and his judgement is almost divine insofar as the characters are unable to question his rulings at the end of the play. Even his apology to Ferdinand in Act IV scene 1 for cruelly enslaving him as a means of testing his love for Miranda is rather half-hearted, as he simply informs him that he should be grateful to have such a wonderful wife. It should, however, also be acknowledged that Prospero is single-handedly responsible for regaining his rightful position and creating unity between Naples and Milan. The two cities would have faced a future of much greater uncertainty had Antonio and Sebastian continued the cycle of usurpations and murders in the pursuit of power. Alonso is made to see the error of his ways and to sue for forgiveness for his actions. Overall, Prospero contains elements of both an agent of moral improvement and an authoritarian judge of others. It is up to students to decide exactly how they think his character is balanced.

Happily ever after?

In Act V scene 1 Gonzalo is unstinting in his praise of the resolution achieved in the play and deems it worthy of permanent record, speaking of inscribing the 'joy' (207) of these scenes of reconciliation on 'lasting pillars' (208). This imagery suggests that Prospero has built an enduring edifice of peace, and that each character has gone through a valuable process of self-analysis, at a time when 'no man was his own' (213). In this sense the process of the play has been a learning one, which emphasises the theme of finding or discovering. Ferdinand's miraculous survival is mentioned, his engagement to Miranda, and also the fact that Prospero regains his dukedom.

Although Gonzalo's positive interpretation is appealing, it is perhaps excessively optimistic. He celebrates Claribel's marriage, despite the uncertainty several different characters have expressed about the wisdom of it. She is still so distant as to be virtually lost to her family, and doubts remain over how willing she was to marry her father's choice of suitor. More generally, the question of whether the happy endings achieved in the play will last depends largely on the good will of Antonio and Sebastian, whose temperaments have not hitherto been reliable. The fact that all the events mentioned by Gonzalo have happened 'in one voyage' (208) increases the sense of miracle surrounding them, but it also aggravates our doubts about whether the good which comes out of the play can be sustained.

Gods, godliness and Christian morality

Like so many of Shakespeare's plays, *The Tempest* is full of references to divinity, hell, the heavens and the devil. In the seventeenth century religion was an intrinsic part of society in a way that it no longer is today. The Church had enormous political power to define social and moral conventions, and playwrights had to be extremely careful to uphold these values if they were to avoid prosecution, or criticism from religious groups like the **Puritans**.

As early as 1579, Stephen Gosson argued in 'The Schoole of Abuse' that audiences imitated what they saw on the stage, and that to present immoral behaviour was consequently to perpetuate it. While the appearance of purpose-built theatres in the Renaissance period made it possible for the first time for playwrights to earn a living by writing professionally, they had to be more alive than ever to the potential dangers — both economic and legal — of offending either royal or popular taste. Thomas Nashe, among other writers of the time, was imprisoned for his part in the authorship of *The Isle of Dogs*, which the authorities deemed to be seditious.

In this context it is hardly surprising that Shakespeare was at pains to present himself as a playwright of impeccable moral integrity. Sir Philip Sidney, writing his *Apologie for Poetrie* (1595) in direct response to Gosson, concurred with the theory that audiences were influenced by what they saw, but maintained that:

> Poetrie euer setteth vertue so out in her best cullours, making Fortune her
> wel-wayting hand-mayd, that one must needs be enamored of her.

Writing as he was under great social pressure, Shakespeare could hardly afford to ignore the moral implications of his plays. As a result he is at great pains in *The Tempest* to emphasise the triumph of good over evil, of order over chaos, truth over deceit. Although it is no simplistic comedy, the play certainly has a strong instructive quality. By foregrounding the themes of divinity and damnation Shakespeare succeeds in emphasising the moral import of the play as well as tackling philosophical issues such as the nature — and limits — of human responsibility and power.

Divinity

There are no explicit references to a Christian God in the play, as this was considered blasphemous and was therefore banned. Indeed, the characters make reference to 'the gods' or other external forces which they believe influence their destiny. In

Act I scene 1 Gonzalo greets the splitting of the ship with a cry of 'The wills above be done' (63), resigning himself to forces greater than himself. He is a fatalistic character who personifies the attitude that human actions are controlled by external sources of authority.

Alonso too learns to accept this point of view, asking whether Miranda is a 'goddess' (V.1.187) and then declaring at the end of the play that 'Some oracle/Must rectify our knowledge' (V.1.244–45). So much beyond belief has occurred that he requires a divine or supernatural force to illuminate its true meaning. Prospero offers to fulfil this explanatory role by telling his life story in his cell. This suggests that he is indeed some sort of divine power in the play who — at least in term's of the play's action — is **omniscient** and **omnipotent**. It is only in the Epilogue, when he is stripped of his magic and power shifts to the audience, that he asks to be released 'by prayer' (16). By this point he has become a supplicant, who must beg for mercy just as others petitioned him earlier in the play.

Caliban exhibits his worrying tendency to idolatry from his first meeting with Stephano and Trinculo. He refers to the 'celestial liquor' borne by 'a brave god' (II.2.115) and thinks his new companions have come from the sky: 'Hast thou not dropped from heaven?' (II.2.34). Later he offers to devote himself to Stephano's divinity: 'I prithee, be my god' (II.2.146). Although Caliban eventually realises 'What a thrice double ass/Was I to take this drunkard for a god,/And worship this dull fool!' (V.1.296–98), the language of divinity infuses his entire relationship with Stephano.

Hell and damnation

When Ferdinand first leaps into the sea he cries out that 'Hell is empty,/And all the devils are here!' (see Ariel's description, I.2.214–15), indicating that he considers the storm to be a work of Satan. Ferdinand is a pious character who assumes that supernatural events are the work of the devil, as most people would have done at the time. His virtuous outlook entitles him to bemoan evil, but Sebastian is in a much weaker position to do so, and there is great irony in Act III scene 3 when he denounces Ariel as a 'fiend' (104); according to Prospero, it is he and Antonio who are 'worse than devils' (37).

Caliban is also referred to as a 'devil' or 'demi-devil' (V.1.272) at several points in the play. In this sense he represents 'the other' — the creature who looks and acts differently, and therefore represents a threat to the established order. He is the son of a witch (women who were believed to have sexual union with Satan himself) and is dark-skinned (blackness was usually associated with evil at that time). We may, however, question the validity of the various labels he is given. One of Shakespeare's greatest villains, Iago from *Othello*, is also termed a 'demi-devil', and there is little comparison to be made between this malignant force for evil and

Caliban. To some extent this illustrates how characters who cannot be categorised according to society's norms are branded as satanic in order to explain away their otherness — an approach that may create a self-fulfilling prophecy whereby characters become evil because this is the way others see them.

Christian allegory

The Tempest is infused with religious imagery, much of which promotes a Christian message that those who have sinned must undergo a period of suffering in order to be received into God's grace once again. Prospero himself has already endured a 12-year penance since being banished from Milan, and acknowledges that he was too deeply involved in the study of magic to carry out his duties to his subjects.

Alonso's repentance grows out of his belief that Ferdinand has died and that his death is Alonso's punishment for his part in usurping Prospero. Only when Alonso has suffered enough to wish himself dead and 'mudded' next to his son (III.3.104) is Ferdinand miraculously restored to him. The fratricidal theme of the play also has strong connections to Christian themes, echoing Cain's murder of his brother Abel in the Old Testament. Furthermore, the banquet which Ariel conjures up in Act III scene 3 can be interpreted as a form of communion; it vanishes when Sebastian steps forward to eat, indicating that he is not yet fit to receive it, having failed to repent adequately for his sins. Miranda too plays a symbolic religious role. She represents virginal innocence and compassion, and intercedes both for the shipwrecked voyagers and for Ferdinand when she fears that her father is treating them cruelly.

Quotations

The best quotations to know are those you have found useful in class discussions and practice essays, and they will require little conscious learning because you are already familiar with them. The most useful additional ones to learn are those which serve more than one purpose, i.e. which can be used to illustrate a theme or image as well as a point about character or dramatic effect. Think about which points each quotation below could be used to support in an examination or coursework essay.

Act I scene 1

What cares these roarers for the name of king? (*Boatswain, ll. 16–17*)

Let's all sink wi'th'King. (*Antonio, l. 59*)

The wills above be done, but I would fain die a dry death. (*Gonzalo, ll. 63–64*)

Act I scene 2

O, I have suffered/With those that I saw suffer! (*Miranda, ll. 5–6*)

I have done nothing but in care of thee... (*Prospero, l. 16*)

'Tis time/I should inform thee farther. (*Prospero, ll. 22–23*)

The hour's now come. (*Prospero, l. 36*)

'Tis far off,/And rather like a dream than an assurance/That my remembrance warrants. (*Miranda, ll. 44–46*)

...rapt in secret studies... (*Prospero, l. 77*)

Dost thou attend me? (*Prospero, l. 78*)

...new created ... (*Prospero, l. 81*)

Good wombs have borne bad sons. (*Miranda, l. 120*)

'Hell is empty,/And all the devils are here!' (*Ariel, ll. 214–15*)

Before the time be out? (*Prospero, l. 246*)

Thou liest, malignant thing! (*Prospero, l. 257*)

A freckled whelp, hag-born — not honoured with/A human shape. (*Prospero, ll. 283–84*)

Thou poisonous slave, got by the devil himself/Upon thy wicked dam, come forth! (*Prospero, ll. 319–20*)

A south-west blow on ye/And blister you all o'er. (*Caliban, ll. 323–24*)

This island's mine, by Sycorax my mother... (*Caliban, l. 331*)

I loved thee,/And showed thee all the qualities o'th'isle... (*Caliban, ll. 336–37*)

I am all the subjects that you have,/Which first was mine own king... (*Caliban, ll. 341–42*)

I have used thee,/Filth as thou art, with human care... (*Prospero, ll. 345–46*)

I had peopled else/This isle with Calibans. (*Caliban, ll. 350–51*)

You taught me language, and my profit on't/Is, I know how to curse. (*Caliban, ll. 363–64*)

I must obey. His art is of such power,/It would control my dam's god Setebos,/And make a vassal of him. (*Caliban, ll. 372–74*)

Where should this music be? I'th'air or th'earth?/It sounds no more; and sure it waits upon/Some god o'th'island. (*Ferdinand, ll. 388–90*)

A thing divine, for nothing natural/I ever saw so noble. (*Miranda, ll. 419–20*)

It goes on, I see,/As my soul prompts it. (*Prospero, ll. 420–21*)

They are both in either's powers. (*Prospero, l. 451*)

There's nothing ill can dwell in such a temple. (*Miranda, l. 458*)

Act II scene 1

You cram these words into mine ears against/The stomach of my sense. (*Alonso, ll. 108–09*)

You rub the sore,/When you should bring the plaster. (*Gonzalo, ll. 140–41*)

I'th'commonwealth I would by contraries/Execute all things. (*Gonzalo, ll. 150–51*)

I would with such perfection govern, sir,/T'excel the Golden Age. (*Gonzalo, ll. 172–73*)

My strong imagination sees a crown/Dropping upon thy head. (*Antonio, ll. 212–13*)

As thou got'st Milan,/I'll come by Naples. (*Sebastian, ll. 296–97*)

Act II scene 2

There would this monster make a man. (*Trinculo, ll. 29–30*)

That's a brave god, and bears celestial liquor. (*Caliban, l. 115*)

I'll show thee every fertile inch o'th'island, and I will kiss thy foot. I prithee, be my god. (*Caliban, ll. 145–46*)

…we will inherit here… (*Stephano, l. 172*)

Act III scene 1

Some kinds of baseness/Are nobly undergone, and most poor matters/Point to rich ends. (*Ferdinand, ll. 2–4*)

O, she is/Ten times more gentle than her father's crabbed… (*Ferdinand, ll. 7–8*)

Poor worm, thou art infected. (*Prospero, l. 31*)

O my father,/I have broke your hest to say so! (*Miranda, ll. 36–37*)

…I'll be your servant/Whether you will or no. (*Miranda, ll. 85–86*)

Act III scene 2

The poor monster's my subject, and he shall not suffer indignity. (*Stephano, ll. 35–36*)

Thou shalt be lord of it, and I'll serve thee. (*Caliban, l. 57*)

She will become thy bed, I warrant,/And bring thee forth brave brood. (*Caliban, ll. 105–06*)

…the isle is full of noises,/Sounds, and sweet airs, that give delight and hurt not. (*Caliban, ll. 136–37*)

…when I waked/I cried to dream again. (*Caliban, ll. 143–44*)

Act III scene 3

If in Naples/I should report this now, would they believe me? (*Gonzalo, ll. 28–29*)

Their manners are more gentle, kind, than of/Our human generation you shall find/Many, nay, almost any. (*Gonzalo, ll. 33–35*)

You are three men of sin… (*Ariel, l. 54*)

I and my fellows/Are ministers of Fate. (*Ariel, ll. 61–62*)

Act IV scene 1

I/Have given you here a third of mine own life… (*Prospero, ll. 2–3*)

All thy vexations/Were but my trials of thy love… (*Prospero, ll. 5–6*)

…she will outstrip all praise,/And make it halt behind her. (*Prospero, ll. 10–11*)

The strongest oaths are straw/To th'fire i'th'blood. (*Prospero, ll. 52–53*)

So rare a wondered father and a wise/Makes this place Paradise. (*Ferdinand, ll. 123–24*)

I had forgot that foul conspiracy/Of the beast Caliban… (*Prospero, ll. 139–40*)

We are such stuff/As dreams are made on; and our little life/Is rounded with a sleep. (*Prospero, ll. 156–58*)

…I feared/Lest I might anger thee. (*Ariel, ll. 168–69*)

A devil, a born devil, on whose nature/Nurture can never stick… (*Prospero, ll. 188–89*)

Let it alone, thou fool! It is but trash. (*Caliban, l. 224*)

Act V scene 1

…time/Goes upright with his carriage. (*Prospero, ll. 2–3*)

…if you now beheld them your affections/Would become tender. (*Ariel, ll. 18–19*)

The rarer action is/In virtue than in vengeance. (*Prospero, ll. 27–28*)

They being penitent,/The sole drift of my purpose doth extend/Not a frown further. (*Prospero, ll. 28–30*)

…this rough magic/I here abjure… (*Prospero, ll. 50–51*)

I'll break my staff,/[…]/And deeper than did ever plummet sound/I'll drown my book. (*Prospero, ll. 54–57*)

I do forgive thee,/Unnatural though thou art. (*Prospero, ll. 78–79*)

All torment, trouble, wonder, and amazement/Inhabits here. (*Gonzalo, ll. 104–05*)

At this time/I will tell no tales. (*Prospero, ll. 128–29*)

...whom to call brother/Would even infect my mouth... (*Prospero, ll. 130–31*)

...was landed/To be the lord on't. (*Prospero, ll. 161–62*)

Though the seas threaten, they are merciful. (*Ferdinand, l. 178*)

MIRANDA: O brave new world,/That has such people in't!
PROSPERO: 'Tis new to thee. (*ll. 183–84*)

...of whom I have/Received a second life... (*Ferdinand, ll. 194–95*)

Let us not burden our remembrances with/A heaviness that's gone (*Prospero, ll. 199–200*)

This thing of darkness I/Acknowledge mine. (*Prospero, ll. 275–76*)

Every third thought shall be my grave. (*Prospero, l. 312*)

Epilogue

As you from crimes would pardoned be,/Let your indulgence set me free.
(*Prospero, ll. 19–20*)

Critical voices

The following well-known critics' comments from the last three centuries show changing attitudes to *The Tempest* and its characters. They offer useful support for your own opinions in a coursework or exam essay, and can provide evidence of opposing views.

...whether or no his [Caliban's] generation can be defended, I leave to philosophy... (John Dryden, 1679)

The highest and lowest characters are brought together, and with what excellence! (Samuel Taylor Coleridge, 1811–12)

Caliban is in some respects a noble being: the poet has raised him far above contempt... (Samuel Taylor Coleridge, 1811–12)

...it is in the soul of man, that still vexed island hung between the upper and the nether world, and liable to incursions from both. (James Russell Lovell, 1870)

The whole play, indeed, is a succession of illusions... (James Russell Lovell, 1870)

...in the *Tempest Period*, man is master of the universe. And — what is here essential — this masterhood of Nature is accompanied by a supreme moral goodness to fellow-man. (Sidney Lanier, 1880)

...the gift of civilisation is turned into a curse... (Richard G. Moulton, 1888)

...nothing, surely, of equal length and variety lives so happily and radiantly as a whole... (Henry James, 1907)

...it is the majesty of art: we *feel* that we are greater than we know. (Arthur Quiller-Couch, 1918)

The pure and impractical is brought into juxtaposition with the practical and impure. (Alfred Harbage, 1947)

We spend our lives partly in a waking world we call normal and partly in a dream world which we create out of our desires. (Northrop Frye, 1948)

...it resembles the story of Adam and Eve, type-story of our troubles. (Nevill Coghill, 1949)

...the development of the action and its final solution are all conjugations of the basic paradigms of classical comedy. (Bernard Knox, 1954)

The Tempest, [is] a Utopia which Shakespeare invented for himself... (Bernard Knox, 1954)

[Prospero is] an imperialist by circumstance, a sadist by disease; and above all, an old man in whom envy and revenge are equally matched... (George Lamming, 1960)

Caliban is his [Prospero's] convert, colonised by language, and excluded by language. (George Lamming, 1960)

The Tempest [is] now unfortunately reduced to an allegory about colonialism... (Brian Vickers, 1993)

Caliban...is another challenge to the humanists' naive belief that the gift of speech is inherently civilising... (Brian Vickers, 1993)

Prospero has given Caliban language; and with it an unstated history of consequences, an unknown history of future intentions. (Jonathan Goldberg, 2001)

Literary terms and concepts

The terms and concepts below have been selected for their relevance to talking and writing about *The Tempest*. It will aid argument and expression to become familiar with them and to use them in your discussion and essays.

allegory symbolic work, in which characters and events can be understood to represent a deeper political, historical or moral meaning

ambiguity capacity of words to have two simultaneous meanings in the same context, either accidentally or, more often, as a deliberate device for enriching the meaning of text. For example, when Sebastian exclaims 'A most high miracle' (V.1.177), he may be truly astounded, or speaking sarcastically

ambivalence	simultaneous coexistence of opposing feelings or attitudes
aside	remark spoken by a character in a play which is shared with the audience but unheard by some or all of the other characters on stage
blank verse	unrhymed **iambic pentameter**, the staple form of Shakespeare plays
caesura	deliberate break in a line of poetry, signified by punctuation
climax	moment of intensity to which a series of actions has been leading
colloquial	informal language of speech rather than that of writing
courtly love	a formal system of love and courtship, governed by gender stereotypes and expectations
crux (pl cruces)	point for debate which is essential for resolving an argument
dénouement	unfolding of the final stages of a plot, when all is revealed; in French, it literally means 'untying'
deus ex machina	literally, the god from the machine; it refers to a supernatural intervention which resolves a difficult situation
didactic	designed to convey an overtly moral or instructive message
dramatic irony	when the audience knows something the character speaking does not, which can create tension or humour and can therefore be a useful element of tragedy or comedy
dystopian	pessimistic inverse of a **utopian** view; the tendency to think the worst of humans and society, and to see society as deeply flawed
elegy	mournful song or poem composed to lament a death
emotive	describes that which arouses an emotional response in the reader or audience
end-stopped	line of poetry which ends with some form of punctuation, creating a pause, e.g. 'Come away, servants, come! I am ready now' (I.2.187)
enjamb(e)ment	run-on instead of **end-stopped** line of poetry, usually to reflect its meaning, e.g. Caliban speaks of Miranda: 'I never saw a woman/But only Sycorax my dam and she' (III.2.101–02)

eponymous	where a name is also used as a title. For example, Othello is the eponymous hero of Shakespeare's play
feminine ending	unstressed syllable at the end of a line of verse
feminism	school of criticism concerned with analysing literature from a female perspective
Freud	twentieth-century scientist who founded the school of psycho-analysis, which was based on the theory that unconscious motives control human behaviour
genre	type or form of writing
Golden Age	this 'first age of man' is described in the works of Ovid as a paradisal period, without war, famine or disease
harpy	a traditionally malevolent, winged, female, mythological creature
hubris	transgressing the laws and commands of the gods, having ignored their warnings
hyperbole	deliberate exaggeration for effect, e.g. 'I had rather crack my sinews, break my back,/Than you should such dishonour undergo' (III.1.26–27)
iambic pentameter	five feet of iambs, i.e. alternating unstressed/stressed syllables; tetrameter has four feet and hexameter (alexandrines) has six
imagery	figurative descriptive language; a pattern of related images that helps to build up mood and atmosphere, and to develop the themes of a literary work
in medias res	beginning a scene or chapter in the middle of an event or dialogue
irony	discrepancy between the actual and implied meaning of language; an amusing or cruel reversal of an outcome expected, intended or deserved; a situation in which one is mocked by fate or the facts
Machiavellian	early sixteenth-century political philosophy proposed by the Italian Niccolò Machiavelli in his book *The Prince*, which recommended ruthless self-interest and unethical methods to gain political power

metaphor	figure of speech in which one thing is described in terms of another, the comparison being implicit, not explicit as in a simile, e.g. Miranda describes her modesty as 'the jewel in my dower' (III.1.54)
metatheatre	style of drama which acknowledges and draws attention to the artificiality of the theatre, the dramatic techniques it uses, and the role of the playwright
micro/ macrocosm	states and occurrences in the individual organism, e.g. violence or conflict, are magnified and reflected in larger contexts, e.g. civil war, tempest
motif	recurring literary, verbal or structural device which develops or reminds the audience of a theme. Ariel's references to time in the opening and closing acts (I.2.240 and V.1.4), for example, emphasise the structure of the play and Shakespeare's conformity to the unity of time
Oedipal	Oedipus was a character from Greek mythology who unknowingly murdered his father and married his mother
omnipotent	all-powerful; refers to the ability of a character or playwright to assume godlike powers over others
omniscient	all-knowing; refers to a character or playwright's godlike knowledge
paradox	self-contradictory statement or state of affairs, e.g. Ferdinand describes how Miranda's presence as he moves logs for Prospero 'makes my labours pleasures' (III.1.7)
pathetic fallacy	attribution of human characteristics to nature or inanimate objects, often to represent the emotional or physical states of human characters, e.g. the tempest represents Prospero's anger
pathos	pity evoked by a situation of suffering and helplessness
peripeteia	sudden reversal of fortune — a good example would be the delight of Stephano and Trinculo at stealing Prospero's rich clothes at the end of Act IV, which soon turns to dismay as they are chased away by spirits in the shape of wild hounds
poetic justice	due allocation of reward and punishment for virtue and vice respectively

post-colonialism	school of criticism which considers texts in the light of global empire-building, and the subsequent return of sovereignty to the indigenous peoples of these countries
post-structuralism	school of criticism, derived from structuralism, which analyses texts by questioning the basis upon which the structures of society's conventions and language have been established
pun	use of a word with double meaning for humorous or ironic effect, e.g. in Act II scene 1, Sebastian claims 'we prosper well in our return' (74–75), unintentionally punning on Prospero, who is indeed responsible for whether they return home
Puritans	group of Protestants in sixteenth- and seventeenth-century England who believed in strict moral and religious discipline
relativism	school of thought which contends that ideas of right and wrong, truth and falsehood change from place to place, and that there can be no single reliable method for judging any person or value as objectively superior to another
Renaissance	originating in Italy, the revival of art and literature in the fifteenth and sixteenth centuries in western Europe, under the influence of classical models
rhetoric	art of persuasion, using emotive language and syntactical devices
rhyming couplet	pair of adjacent rhyming lines
romance	story of love and heroism, deriving from medieval court life and fairy tale
seven deadly sins	according to the medieval Catholic Church, the following sins were mortal and led straight to hell: pride, envy, gluttony, lechery, avarice, wrath and sloth. Many contemporary and later literary works include these sins symbolically or thematically
simile	comparison introduced by 'as' or 'like', e.g. Prospero describes how his trust for Antonio 'Like a good parent, did beget of him/A falsehood in its contrary' (I.2.94–95)
soliloquy	speech by character alone on stage which reveals his/her thoughts
sources	stories or inspirations, drawn from history, mythology or other literary works, which writers build into their own artistic creation

stoicism	ancient Greek school of philosophy which propounded the theory that happiness can only be achieved by accepting that good fortune and misfortune are beyond human control, e.g. in *The Tempest*, Gonzalo is quick to resign himself to fate as he dives into the sea in Act I scene 1, asserting: 'The wills above be done'
structuralism	school of criticism which analyses texts according to the premise that human society is a network of interrelated elements which yield significant patterns
superlative	exaggerated description usually expressing admiration; the grammatical form which expresses the highest degree of comparison, e.g. when Gonzalo claims in Act II scene 1 that 'The air breathes on us here most sweetly'
suspension of disbelief	Coleridge used this expression to explain how an audience does not apply the normal rules of realism when watching drama but has a 'poetic faith' in theatrical conventions and chooses to believe in the fictional world
symbol	object, person or event which represents something more than itself, e.g. the sea
theme	abstract idea or issue explored in a literary work, distinct from the content
tragi-comedy	literary genre which combines aspects of tragedy and comedy
unities (the)	three principles of dramatic composition, deriving from Aristotle, whereby a play should consist of one related series of actions, occur within one day, and happen in one location. Shakespeare pays respect to the unities in *The Tempest* and in the second half of *Othello*
utopian	term deriving from Sir Thomas More's *Utopia* (1516), used to describe a perfect place or state, or the view that such a place or state exists
verisimilitude	appearance of truth or reality, which often masks a different version of events
verse	language organised according to its rhythmical qualities into regular patterns of metre and set out in lines

Questions & Answers

Essay questions, specimen plans and notes

Coursework essays

Below are some possible titles which would be appropriate for a coursework essay.

1 Explore how Shakespeare examines the themes of repentance and reconciliation in *The Tempest*.

You should refer to the following in your answer:

- the relationship between the themes of repentance and reconciliation and the play's genre
- the key scenes which address the themes of repentance and reconciliation
- the dramatic impact these scenes would have on the audience
- how the original audience would have responded differently from a modern one
- how issues linked to repentance and reconciliation are revealed to the audience through characters, imagery and language
- how Prospero contributes to the portrayal of these themes
- how themes of repentance and reconciliation have been commented on by various critics
- the 'message' of the play
- Prospero's motives for forgiving the other characters
- how convincing you found the repentance of different characters
- your own view on how the themes of repentance and reconciliation are shown and developed in the play

Examiners noted that weaker candidates were too colloquial in their use of language, and referred to the 'book' or 'novel' instead of the 'play'. Stronger candidates were aware of the relationship between particular scenes and the whole play, and also showed awareness of the particular Assessment Objectives which were being tested. The best candidates integrated their quotations into the structure of their essays, used technical vocabulary and provided close analysis. They also treated the play as a dramatic text and were aware of the critical context of the play without substituting others' ideas for their own. Successful candidates had a clear line of argument.

(Source: AQA Specification A, June 2004)

Further questions

2 Explore how Shakespeare examines the themes of magic and illusion in *The Tempest*. Compare your interpretation of *The Tempest* with that of other critics.

3 What interests you most about *The Tempest*? Give a detailed analysis of the complexities and challenges of the play as far as a modern audience is concerned.

4 What similarities and contrasts are drawn in the play between the world of the island and Italy?

5 Explore the character of Prospero, showing how he develops through the play and saying how convincing you find him.

6 Explore the character of Prospero, tracing and accounting for his behaviour throughout the play.

7 Choose any two characters who offer interesting points for comparison and contrast. Write a study of their roles in the play and your response to them as characters. (Suggestions: Prospero and Miranda; Ariel and Caliban; Alonso and Antonio; Gonzalo and Ferdinand.)

8 Is it significant that there is only one female character in the play? Consider how Shakespeare portrays Miranda, examining the way she is characterised, and what her function in the play is.

9 Does Shakespeare succeed in individualising the minor characters? Consider four or five examples to support your answer.

10 Write about the use of imagery in *The Tempest* and its contribution to the overall effect of the play.

11 What have you gained in your knowledge of Shakespeare and his period by your study of this play and its critics?

Exam essays

The exemplar essay questions which follow can be used for planning practice and/or full essay writing within the time limit, with or without the text. Many have been previously set by different exam boards for various specifications. In each of the three sections there are some essay titles with suggestions for ideas to include in a plan, and some with examiners' notes and guidance on how to approach the question. Two questions are provided with sample student answers. Remember to write about the play and the audience, not the book and the reader, and try to visualise how it would appear on stage and how it would sound; the drama and the poetry are essential elements of the written text you are being asked to respond to. Here are the questions to address when analysing drama text passages:

- Is it all verse, all prose, or a mixture?
- Is it primarily looking forward to something which is to come, or looking backwards to explain or reinforce a previous event?
- Are there any entrances or exits, and what effect do they have if so?
- Look at stage directions. What are the visual effects of the position of props and the actions being performed?
- Comment on the imagery and relate it to other usages and its link with themes.
- Is there a dominant or silent presence or one who is given relatively few lines?
- Is there any irony or dramatic irony? Who knows what at this stage?
- Where is the audience's sympathy, and why?
- Is the passage similar to or a contrast to another episode?

- How does the language and its tone reveal character, and how does it affect the audience's feelings about something or someone?
- How does the scene add to plot and character, themes and language? Why is it there?

Whole-text questions: open text

Note: some of the questions in this section could be suitable as closed-text questions.

1 What do you find interesting about Shakespeare's presentation of Prospero in the play? You may confine yourself to two episodes or range more widely, if you prefer.

AO1–3   Detailed analysis and exploration of the way the writer has constructed the drama with close attention to language and presentation of Prospero; critical vocabulary tellingly used.

AO4   Mature and confident judgement; clear, coherent argument; focus is on 'you find interesting'.

(Source: top band descriptors, AQA Specification A, January 2004)

Possible ideas to include in a plan

- explore contradictory nature of Prospero's character; shows vengefulness and mercy, kindness and cruelty at different points in the play
- analyse different critical interpretations of Prospero and how these have changed historically
- consider different sorts of interaction Prospero has with different characters
- emphasise role of Shakespeare in creating Prospero's character by conscious choices he makes as a writer
- consider parallels between Prospero's role and that of Shakespeare, as playwright
- consider whether Prospero develops as a character during the play, and in what ways
- explore Prospero's various roles in the play
- emphasise your personal response to Prospero, in the context of alternative readings

Further questions

2 'Society in miniature.' How far is this your view of the island as represented in *The Tempest*?

In your answer you should:

- **explore the preservation of the various factions of society, including the role of Prospero**
- **comment on relevant issues such as rank and the importance of ceremony**

3 Discuss the theme of redemption through suffering in *The Tempest*.

In your answer you should consider:

- **to what extent the major characters find redemption through their experiences on the island**

■ the significance of spiritual and religious imagery

4 'Prospero is a tyrant and a control freak.' How far do you agree with this view?

5 What is the significance of music in the play as a whole?

6 What is the effect of the time scheme utilised in the play?

7 How significant is the island as a setting for the play's action?

8 To what extent do you think *The Tempest* can be described accurately as a tragi-comedy?

9 How does your knowledge of colonialism affect your reading of *The Tempest*?

10 Do you agree that *The Tempest* is most usefully interpreted as a Christian allegory?

11 Examine Shakespeare's treatment of the theme of usurpation in *The Tempest*.

12 Discuss Shakespeare's treatment of forgiveness and judgement in the play.

13 'Prospero is merely a surrogate for Shakespeare, authoring his own story as he goes along.' How far do you agree with this view?

Whole-text questions: closed text

Note: some of the questions in this section could be suitable as open-text questions.

1 'The Prospero–Caliban relationship can be seen as a reflection of European man's first encounters with the American Indian.' How helpful is this interpretation to what you take *The Tempest* to be about?

Notes on the task

Candidates must engage with a controversial but central issue of *The Tempest*, expressing their own views but being aware of other possible perspectives (AO4). Their answers must be based on a sound knowledge of the text (AO2ii) and on the ability to analyse the techniques used by Shakespeare in establishing the relationship between Prospero and Caliban (AO3); they will also have to evaluate the significance of key cultural and historical influences on the way the play may be understood (AO5ii).

Answers that are penetrating and original will fall into the top band, and will display these qualities:

AO1   A sophisticated level of understanding and insight communicated with flair and deftness.

AO2ii   A strong degree of textual knowledge, and a detailed perception of the structure of the plot and the workings of the relationship between Prospero and Caliban.

AO3   Convincing analysis of Shakespeare's use of language and dramatic strategies to convey Prospero's and Caliban's respective positions.

AO4   A mature sense of individual opinion and an intelligent, personal response to the issues arising from the relationship between Prospero and Caliban in a colonial context; a full engagement with the question which invites awareness that perceptions may vary.

AO5ii   Confidence in evaluating contextual influences such as perceptions of how far members of a Jacobean or modern audience may have been/are aware of colonial issues.

(Source: OCR Specification, 2000)

2 'In *The Tempest* revenge and reconciliation are in permanent tension.' How helpful do you find this view of the play?

Answers that are penetrating and original will fall into the top band, and will display these qualities:

AO1   Lucid expression in a relevant and well-organised answer.

AO2ii   Some clear sense of, and commentary upon, the relationship between issues appropriate to this question in *The Tempest* and other relevant texts.

AO3   Perceptive and detailed insight into the themes of revenge and reconciliation, with sensitive analysis of the motivation of Prospero and other relevant characters, and close reference to the text.

AO4   Mature and thoughtful response to the play's exploration of these themes, informed by an awareness that different interpretations are possible, indeed likely.

AO5ii   Good understanding of Elizabethan/Jacobean attitudes to revenge and reconciliation, looking also at the dramatic means by which the possibility of either is achieved.

(Source: OCR Specification, 2000)

Further questions

3 Explore the significance of Ferdinand and Miranda as 'lost' children.

4 'This island's mine by Sycorax, my mother,/Which thou tak'st from me.' Do you agree with Caliban?

5 'Though the seas threaten, they are merciful': how does the play explore themes of justice and forgiveness? In your answer you should consider the 'high wrongs' Prospero has suffered, his treatment of those who have injured him, and Shakespeare's presentation of the natural world as a symbol and agent of reconciliation.

6 What do the comic episodes, involving Caliban, Stephano and Trinculo, contribute to the total dramatic effect of *The Tempest?* In your answer you should consider the following:

- the relationship of these scenes to the play's wider themes
- dialogue, and any effects of language
- actions, properties, costume and use of the performing space

7 In what ways have you found *The Tempest* interesting as a play for dramatic performance? In your answer you may wish to discuss any of the following and other relevant comments on the play as a work of theatre:

- the comic interludes
- Caliban, Ariel and the spirits
- magic and music
- the sea, the tempest and the island
- Prospero's books and staff
- the language of the play

8 How far do you agree with Prospero's assertion that 'The rarer action is/In virtue than in vengeance'? Explore the relevance of this comment to the play's themes.

9 Is there any evidence in the play to support the view that usurpation can sometimes be justified?

10 Gonzalo says that the island is 'lush' and fertile. Antonio thinks it is 'tawny' and barren. Whose attitude to the island is right?

11 Northrop Frye argued that, in watching *The Tempest*, 'We spend our lives partly in a waking world we call normal and partly in a dream world which we create out of our desires.' How does the distinction between fantasy and reality affect your interpretation of the play?

12 Explore the different uses and meanings of the word 'Nature' in the play.

Passage-based essay questions

The question you choose may direct you to a prescribed passage or ask you to select your own. Either way you will need to show your knowledge of the whole play as well as your response to and analysis of a particular sequence. Careful selection of passages is crucial to ensure the relevance and success of the essay; the passages you like or are most familiar with are not necessarily the most appropriate for a particular title. Do not waste time paraphrasing what happens in the scene or the content of the speech or dialogue; just give a quick summary of its setting and context, along the lines of who is present and why, what has just happened, what will follow, and what its dramatic purpose is.

Examiners advise that reference to the rest of the work should be as much as 60% of the essay even for a passage-based question. Focus closely on the passage(s) but also relate the content and/or language to elsewhere in the text, backwards and forwards, and link your comments to the overall themes and/or structure of the play. Include references to character, event, theme and language, and ask how the extract modifies or adds to our understanding so far, and how typical it is of the work as a whole. Think about reader/audience reaction, using your own as the basis for your response.

Passage-based questions: prescribed

1 Look again at Act I scene 2, from about line 410, when Miranda says 'What is't? A spirit?' to the end of the scene at the stage direction 'Exeunt', after Prospero says 'Come, follow! (to Miranda) Speak not for him.'

Explore the dramatic significance of this episode within the play.

AO1–3 Detailed analysis and exploration of the way the writer has constructed the episode with close attention to language and dramatic significance; critical vocabulary tellingly used.

AO4 Mature and confident judgement; clear coherent argument; focus is on explore.

(Source: top band descriptors, AQA Specification A, January 2004 specimen materials)

Possible ideas to include in a plan

- it is the first meeting of Miranda and Ferdinand
- there is tension between the two male figures in Miranda's life (future husband and father)
- relate to subsequent episodes, where Prospero and Ferdinand are reconciled to one another
- comment on conventions of courtly love, and the idea of love at first sight
- consider gender roles, and the context of the play
- relevant themes are family, authority, service, love
- consider role of magic on the island, as a means of control and of wonder
- comment on Miranda's relative innocence and inexperience
- examine Prospero's motivations for how he behaves in this scene
- consider the consequences of the match between Miranda and Ferdinand after the action of the play is over
- consider how the scene might be staged, or interpreted in different ways

Further questions

2 Remind yourself of Prospero's lengthy explanation of past events in Act I scene 2. How effective is it as a dramatic device, and how important is it to our understanding of the play?

3 Analyse Prospero's speech after the masque beginning 'Our revels now are ended'. What is its dramatic effect, and how does it relate to the main themes of the play?

4 Remind yourself of Ferdinand and Miranda's courtship scene in Act III scene 1. What do you think this contributes to our understanding of gender issues in the play?

5 Look again at Ariel's speech to the 'three men of sin' in Act III scene 3, and Prospero's immediate response to it. Using this speech as a starting point, consider the importance of magic in the play as a whole.

6 Look again at Caliban's conversation with Prospero, beginning in Act I scene 2, line 322 up until 375. What does this passage contribute to your understanding of the themes of slavery and exploitation in the play?

7 'The masque is unnecessary and even disruptive.' Look again at the masque scene and explain why you agree or disagree with this view.

8 Look again at Prospero's exchange with Ariel in Act V scene 1, beginning 'Dost thou think so, spirit?' (line 19) and ending at line 87. How does it illuminate the themes of revenge, repentance and reconciliation in the play?

9 Remind yourself of the tempest scene at the start of the play. Using this as a starting point, discuss how it relates to the central themes of the play, and our understanding of its characters.

10 Look again at Prospero's Epilogue. Using this as a starting point, explore the themes of magic and illusion in the play.

11 Reread Stephano and Trinculo's first meeting with Caliban, from Act II scene 2, line 18, up until line 146. Comment on the significance of this passage to the language of the play, its characterisation and the development of the plot.

Passage-based questions: selected

1 Select and analyse a sequence which explores the relationship between Prospero and Miranda.

Possible ideas to include in a plan

- Prospero is an authoritarian father
- Miranda is, generally, a humble and obedient daughter
- the play reflected the perspective of a patriarchal society
- Prospero vacillates between being indulgent ('I have done nothing but in care of thee,/Of thee, my dear one' (l.2.16–17)) and stern ('What, I say,/My foot my tutor?' (l.2.469–70))
- relevant themes are family, authority, service, love
- Prospero's attitude to chastity in Act IV shows importance of female virginity on wedding night
- Prospero treats Miranda as a 'gift' or object, to be traded for political advantage
- Prospero's long speech in Act I scene 2 reveals that he has kept Miranda ignorant of past events for 12 years
- Miranda's confident, forthright speech to Caliban shows she is assertive and has learned much from her father
- both Prospero and Miranda are superhuman characters, though in different ways; as such, they both inspire amazement, devotion and worship

Further questions

2 Select and analyse two passages which illuminate Prospero's relationship with Miranda.

3 Select two passages as a starting point and explain the dramatic significance of the Caliban/Stephano/Trinculo sub-plot.

4 Coleridge once claimed that 'Caliban is in some respects a noble being: the poet has raised him far above contempt'. Select two scenes from the play which help you explore this view.

5 James Russell Lovell wrote that 'The whole play, indeed, is a succession of illusions....' Select two passages which explore the importance of illusion in the play.

6 Select two scenes which show contrasting aspects to Prospero's character and explain which of these seems to you to be most characteristic of him.

Sample essays

Below are two sample essays of different types written by different students. Both of them have been assessed as falling within the top band. You can judge them against the Assessment Objectives for this text for your exam board and decide on the mark you think each deserves and why. You will also be able to see ways in which each could be improved in terms of content, style and accuracy.

Sample essay 1

Reread Act V scene 1. In what ways do you find this an effective ending to the play? In your answer you should:

- **look closely at the language and tone that the characters use**
- **explain your own views on how Shakespeare brings the play to an end**
- **comment on the place of relevant issues such as justice and closure**

Some critics find the ending to *The Tempest* problematic, while others believe it fits with the rest of the play. These opinions, however, often depend on the context the play is considered in. A modern audience will react very differently to it than a Shakespearean audience, for example.

In terms of the language used by the different characters, it is clear that Prospero is in charge of the scene. He speaks many more lines than any other character, and organises the reconciliation of the group with his magic. He does, however, use less threatening language than he has used earlier in the play. He declares that he will 'break my staff' and 'drown my book', which shows that he realises that he must give up his magical powers if he is to create a lasting peace.

Alonso seems to be very repentant indeed. He asks 'forgiveness' of Miranda, and returns Prospero's dukedom to him. He marvels at the amazing events of the final scene, and seems very happy that Ferdinand and Miranda are to be married. Gonzalo is a good and innocent character who helped save Prospero and Miranda when they were abandoned at sea many years before. He is therefore even more excited about the situation, and cries 'Amen' at the miracles which he has seen take place.

Perhaps most problematic is the fact that characters like Antonio and Sebastian hardly say anything at all. Seeing as they are supposed to be repenting for their crimes, the audience may well be concerned that their silence means they are unhappy with the way Prospero is treating them, and that the peace we see at the end of the play will not last long. Sebastian even whispers 'The devil speaks in him', as if he thinks Prospero is an evil spirit, so he obviously is not entirely happy.

It is true as well that Prospero is not as humble as he could be in the final scene. He says of Caliban 'This thing of darkness I/Acknowledge mine', but he still calls him a 'misshapen knave', and sends him to tidy his cell as a punishment. Caliban may regret that he has tried to usurp Prospero, but it seems that this is only because he's been caught. He does not apologise for what he has done, and is more worried that 'I shall be pinched to death'. It is certainly interesting to see Prospero begging the audience for its appreciation and 'mercy' at the end of the play, when he has lost his magical powers. It is difficult to imagine how he will behave back in Italy when he does not have total control over all his enemies.

Some critics argue that the silences and unresolved difficulties at the end of the play ruin an otherwise 'happy' ending, which would be more suitable for *The Tempest*. However, I believe that the ending Shakespeare has chosen is most effective because he does not intend to conform to the conventions of comedy. The play is a romance, not a comedy, which means it is optimistic without necessarily having a totally joyful ending. In fact, Shakespeare explores lots of important issues like power, responsibility and revenge, and a comedy might ignore the importance of these issues by suggesting that all the characters are entirely pleased with how the play has ended. Because of this, the play does not have as much closure as you might expect. Instead of being a total end to the conflict of the play, most of the characters are starting a whole new life once they return to Italy. We do not yet know how Antonio and Sebastian will respond to their punishment, and whether they will try to take revenge on Prospero.

It is true that justice has been restored to a large extent in the final act of the play. Stephano and Trinculo are punished for their rebellion, and Alonso's murder has been prevented by Prospero too. Prospero himself has regained his dukedom, but it could be argued that the rules of justice don't apply equally to all the characters. For example, we are not told what Caliban's fate will be, and Antonio's comment that he would be 'marketable' suggests that he may be taken back to Europe as a slave. This is hardly justice for someone who is a native of the island. Another of Prospero's servants, Ariel, is allowed to 'Be free', but this is only because he has obeyed all his master's commands. In actual fact, the justice handed out at the end of the play is Prospero's justice, and our feelings about him will obviously affect whether we believe that the different characters' fates are fair.

Overall I think the ending of *The Tempest* is very effective. It resolves lots of the main issues in the play, but Shakespeare does not try to make out that everything is perfect. Prospero is at the centre of the play's conclusion, as he has been at the centre of the whole play, so it is important to see his plans finally being completed. It is clear from the different characters' language and behaviour that each one of them feels differently about the way the play has turned out, but this is exactly the point: the play's complexity is what makes it interesting, and the awkward justice and sense of some unresolved problems make it the fascinating narrative that it is.

Sample essay 2

'Despite being the only woman on the island, Miranda is one of Shakespeare's strongest female characters.' How far do you agree that Miranda is a strong female character?

In your answer you should:

- set out clearly the arguments for and against this claim
- explain your own views about Shakespeare's presentation of Miranda
- comment on the place of relevant issues such as marriage, duty and independence

Because Miranda is the only woman on the island she is obviously the focus of those who want to consider the gender issues of the play. However, critics have very divided views about the subject, with some thinking of her as a weak and subservient character and others suggesting that she is a feminist icon in many ways.

Women in Shakespeare's time were discriminated against, and would not have taken a very active role in public life. They were expected to be subservient to men and to obey their fathers or husbands. It could be argued that Miranda is a very good daughter as she obviously obeys Prospero for the most part, and he calls her 'a cherubin'.

However, Miranda is not a woman who lacks spirit. She is very disrespectful of Caliban, and calls him an 'Abhorrèd slave'. She also goes against Prospero's wishes by telling Ferdinand her name, and getting engaged secretly. This shows that she knows her own mind, and is happy to make decisions which would normally be left to the man of the family. In fact, Miranda even goes so far as to tell her father not to be so harsh on Ferdinand when he first captures him, before Prospero shouts 'What, I say,/My foot my tutor?' This shows that he expects his daughter to be totally obedient to him, and he is very unimpressed by her disobedience.

Miranda can therefore be seen as a woman who does not conform to the norms of contemporary Italian society. On the other hand, she is not always as gutsy as this. Despite the fact that she says she has never seen another woman, she is certainly aware that females are expected to be chaste, as she says to Ferdinand that her 'modesty' is 'the jewel in my dower'.

Prospero also treats her like his possession when he eventually agrees that Ferdinand can marry Miranda. This is as you would expect it to be in Shakespearean times, with the husband and father discussing the future of the woman behind her back. Prospero says that she has been 'worthily purchased' by Ferdinand, and suggests that she is 'my rich gift', which he is giving away. This shows that Prospero thinks that he has complete control over her, as if she were just an object. This would suggest that Miranda is not as independent as she sometimes seems, and that she is only allowed to be educated and talkative in public because Prospero lets her.

I think Shakespeare is deliberately saying that Miranda's role as a woman on the island is complex. As a character, she is certainly very interesting and intelligent, but she must also give in to the rules of society, if she is going to get along in life. What is so complex about her character is that she holds a lot of power over all the male characters, but they ultimately have the power to command her. For example, Stephano wants to make her his queen, and Caliban tries to rape her, which shows that she has sexual appeal and power over those men. But this attractive power is also dangerous because she needs to be protected by Prospero as a result of it. In this way, she is physically weak, and reliant on men for protection.

Miranda can never be independent because of the society she has been born into. Because of this, she must be as dutiful and obedient as she needs to be. Nevertheless, she clearly has lots of admiration from the other people in that society, so she should certainly not be considered weak. Perhaps one problem she encounters as such a beautiful and intelligent woman is that she seems too perfect. Because everyone thinks that she is a 'goddess', or a 'nonpareil', this means that there is lots of pressure on her to conform to a female stereotype of perfection, rather than being her own person. Nevertheless, these favourable descriptions also suggest that Shakespeare wants her to be interpreted positively, and the audience of a production would find it difficult not to like her.

I think that Miranda can be considered as a strong female character in many ways, but she is limited by the men around her too. She shows plenty of examples of spirited behaviour, which suggest that she would be even more of a strong character if she lived in a different society. However, because she realises that she must ultimately do what her father says, she is wise enough to realise that she can get her own way by being obedient, rather than trying to rebel. Perhaps she is not a 'strong' character like Lady Macbeth or Cleopatra, but Miranda does not seem to feel like she needs to take society on head-on, like those two characters. In fact, she ends the play very happily, and gets what she wants, which is another sign of a strong character. Although she marries someone her father approves of, Ferdinand is also the person who she most wants to marry. In this sense, she is a strong character, who also fulfils the duties expected of her as a woman in that day and age.

Further study

Articles

Skura, M. A. (1989) 'Discourse and the individual: the case of colonialism in *The Tempest*', in *Shakespeare Quarterly*, 40:1, John Hopkins University Press.

Thornton Burnett, M. (1997) '"Strange and woonderfull syghts": *The Tempest* and discourses of monstrosity', in *Shakespeare Survey*, 50, Cambridge University Press.

Books

Bate, J. (1993) *Shakespeare and Ovid*, Clarendon Press.

Bloom, H. (2000) *The Tempest* (Modern Critical Interpretations), Chelsea House Publishers.

Brown, P. (1985) '"This thing of darkness I acknowledge mine": *The Tempest* and the discourse of colonialism', in Jonathan Dollimore and Alan Sinfield (eds), *Political Shakespeare: New Essays in Cultural Materialism*, Manchester University Press.

Bullough, G. (ed.) (1975) *Narrative and Dramatic Sources of Shakespeare*, Vol. 8, Routledge.

Eastman, A. M. and Harrison, G. B. (eds) (1964) *Shakespeare's Critics from Jonson to Auden*, University of Michigan Press.

Gillies, J. (1994) *Shakespeare and the Geography of Difference*, Cambridge University Press.

Goldberg, J. (2002) *The Generation of Caliban*, Ronsdale Press.

Greenblatt, S. J. (1976) 'Learning to curse: aspects of linguistic colonialism in the sixteenth century', in Fredi Chiappelli (ed.), *First Images of America*, Vol. 2, University of California Press.

Knight, G. Wilson (1932) *The Shakespearean Tempest*, Oxford University Press.

Mannoni, O. (1950) *Prospero and Caliban: The Psychology of Colonialism*, tr. Pamela Powesland, Praeger.

Mason Brown, V. and Vaughan, A. T. (1990) *Shakespeare's Caliban: A Cultural History*, Cambridge University Press.

Mason Brown, V. and Vaughan, A. T. (eds) (1998) *Critical Essays on Shakespeare's 'The Tempest'*, G. K. Hall.

Palmer, D. J. (ed.) (1968) *The Tempest: A Casebook*, Macmillan.

Palmer, D.J. (ed.) (1971) *Shakespeare's Later Comedies*, Penguin.

Smith, H. (1972) *Shakespeare's Romances*, Anderson, Ritchie and Simon.

Tillyard, E. M. W. (1938) *Shakespeare's Last Plays*, Chatto and Windus.

Tillyard, E. M. W. (1943) *The Elizabethan World Picture*, Chatto and Windus.

Traversi, D. (1955) *Shakespeare: The Last Plays*, Stanford University Press.

Films

The Tempest has proved a popular subject for filmmakers, and has been adapted and used as an inspiration for several celluloid productions. Very few of them stick closely to Shakespeare's text, so these films are most useful as an introduction to the many different interpretations of the play. Some memorable ones include:

1956: *Forbidden Planet,* despite being futuristic, is dated in terms of its outlook, but makes good use of music and special effects.

1979: Derek Jarman's 'queer' reading of the play, starring Heathcote Williams as Prospero and Toyah Willcox as Miranda, includes Gothic and Baroque elements in a highly stylised and sexualised production.

1980: the BBC version, directed by John Gorrie, is a fairly unspectacular production, which takes few risks with the play but likewise offers little fresh insight into it.

1982: Paul Mazursky's version, starring John Cassavettes and Susan Sarandon, is a modern and thought-provoking production, if rather a loose adaptation.

1991: *Prospero's Books*, directed by Peter Greenaway and starring John Gielgud, is another adaptation which explores many of the issues surrounding magic, illusion, reality and authority without adhering too closely to Shakespeare's text. It is creative and worthwhile viewing.

1992: *The Animated Tales.* The animated *The Tempest* is part of a collection of four of Shakespeare's best-loved plays. Although it cuts Shakespeare's text quite severely, the form seems appropriate for such a fantastical play.

Internet

There is now a vast number of sites on the internet with useful material on Shakespeare and *The Tempest*. Google is an effective search engine for material on the play, particularly if you can modify your search with key words like 'redemption', 'illusion', 'betrayal', or the names of key characters or themes. A Google search for 'post-colonial readings of *The Tempest*' returns nearly 40,000 references, for example. Although the standard of internet resources is improving all the time, remember that the quality of information available on the net is highly variable. Websites set up and close down with bewildering rapidity, and material is not always accurate. Some websites also charge for access to their resources, and it is difficult to judge whether or not they provide good value before parting with money. Similar material can often be found for free if you are patient and thorough in your use of search engines.

- **http://shakespeare.palomar.edu/** (Mr William Shakespeare and the Internet) is one of the best Shakespeare sites. It includes general information and an extensive set of links to other sites, many of which include the full text of some or all of the plays, listed at **http://shakespeare.palomar.edu/works.htm**. Most of these have some form of search engine which allows the text to be searched for words and phrases.

As far as *The Tempest* is concerned, there are a number of sites, and subsections of more general Shakespeare sites, which are of particular interest:

- **www.sparknotes.com/shakespeare/tempest/** is a good introductory site, with the full text, notes and a search engine.
- **www.cliffsnotes.com** provides similar resources to sparknotes, with links to a range of background material and critical essays on the play's characters and themes.
- **www.absoluteshakespeare.com/guides/tempest/essay/tempest_essay.htm** leads you to Coleridge's famous essay on the play, as well as other resources.
- **http://faculty.pittstate.edu/~knichols/colonial3a.html** is an extremely interesting site that addresses post-colonial aspects of the play and provides numerous links to other useful sites and documents.

Images from various productions of *The Tempest* can be found by entering the names of particular characters into Google's image search, along with the word 'Shakespeare'. Artists' impressions of the play and its characters, as well as postcards of productions and characters through the ages, are available by following the excellent links at:

- **http://shakespeare.emory.edu/**

Other useful websites:

- **www.shakespeares-globe.org/** is the official website of the reconstructed Globe Theatre.
- **www.bl.uk/treasures/shakespeare/homepage.html** offers a quarto view of Shakespeare's works.
- **www.shakespeare.org.uk** is the site of the Shakespeare Birthplace Trust.